Unknown Down

A Cold War Incident
Involving UFOs over South Florida
and the Subsequent Cover-Up by the U.S. Military

Lori,

So glad we're working together and looking forward to the journey!

Jack R[illegible]

Unknown Down

A Cold War Incident
Involving UFOs over South Florida
and the Subsequent Cover-Up by the U.S. Military

By Jack Roth
as told by Bill Schroeder

Foreword by Maurizio Baiata

Unknown Down

Edited by Michael Candelaria and Jon Sumple

Front and Back Cover Design by Joe Mandia

Library of Congress Cataloging-in-Publication Data

Roth, Jack.
Unknown Down: A Cold War Incident Involving UFOs over
South Florida and the Subsequent Cover-Up by the U.S. Military /
Jack Roth. — 1st ed.

CIP Data Available Upon Request.

ISBN 978-1-6827-3737-8

DISCLAIMER: Some of the names in this book have been changed in order to protect the privacy of the witnesses.

First Edition
Printed in the United States of America

Special thanks to Lori Wagner and Jon Sumple for helping me get this project completed on schedule. A sincere "thank you" also goes out to Dennis Force, Robert Salas, Chase Kloetzke, Stanton Friedman, Bob King, Robert Halpern, Francis Ridge, Gerald Flood and Arthur D. Jones for their willingness to talk about their experiences and add intelligent insight into the discussion of UFOs and the phenomenon's significance to the human race.

Bill Schroeder and I would like to dedicate this book to all of the UFO experiencers out there – both civilian and military – who have had to endure the negative consequences associated with the U.S. government's long-standing policy of UFO secrecy and denial.

Table of Contents

I knew very little
When I met them that night
I was aware but unknowing
Till that moment of flight

They came from somewhere
A long ways away
We were destined to meet
In an unusual way

It was my mission that night
To watch Florida skies
A mission accomplished
With electronic eyes

Then they appeared
To my comrades and me
The speed and aerobatics
They were something to see

And we watched them all night
As they moved through the skies
They ignored us and teased us
And made us all wise

I learned a great lesson
That night in the Keys
There are many more out there
Then just you and me

BILL SCHROEDER
March 31, 2016

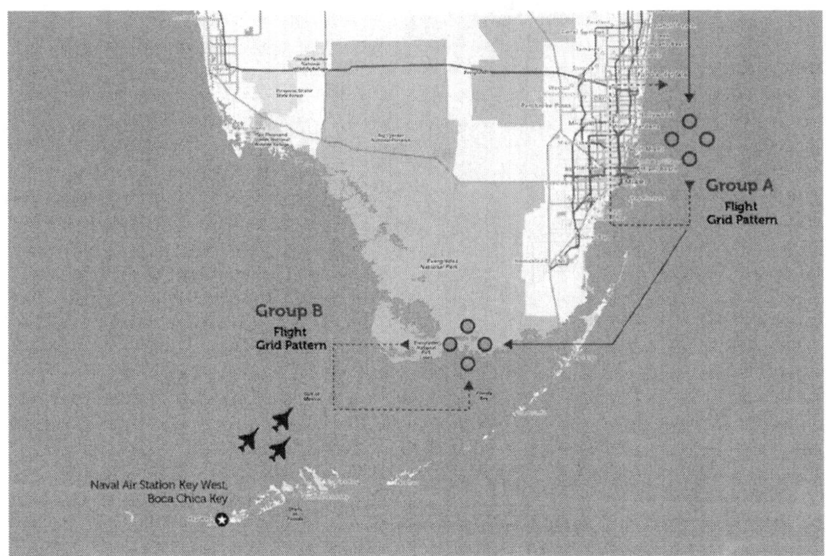

Initial trajectory of the flight pattern for the two UFO groups (A and B) tracked over South Florida on the night of March 31, 1967.

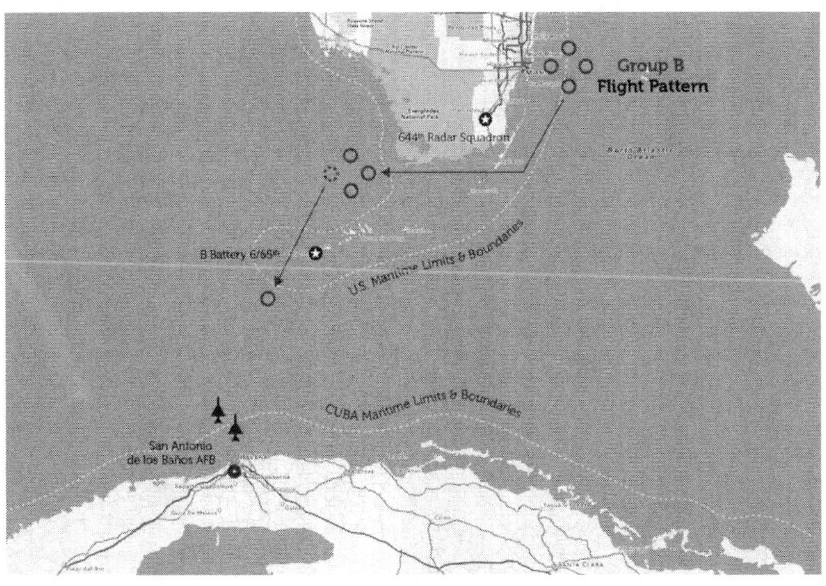

Full trajectory of Group B and the break out of one of the UFOs towards Cuban air space during the early morning hours of April 1, 1967.

Foreword

By Maurizio Baiata
Investigative Journalist and Author

When it comes to the definition of UFOs, I prefer to use the following: UFOs are a product of unknown intelligence in possession of unknown motivations and power. I consider this an effective and grounded definition of a phenomenon characterized by countless sightings and even more theories. But does this definition stand up to the scrutiny given by reading *Unknown Down*? Probably not. It crumbles before the scrutiny of a discipline that cannot be rooted in a rational belief system, since one must extend the human mind to a stellar distance and then, with much difficulty, return to this small earthly world. Then, and only then, can a person get closer to understanding the nature of this complex mystery.

Approaching and understanding such a phenomenon can be likened more to the romantic idea of the *1968 Summer of Love* than to the constricted boundaries of mainstream science. Author Jack Roth works on the assumption that knowing and believing represent odd partners in a super-complex game, played by "we the people" on one side and by an intricate mosaic of quasi-dark powers on the other. Many dedicated researchers risk their professional reputations, and sometimes even their lives, painstakingly investigating and often struggling to ascertain the facts and consequences associated with UFO-related events, including the deeply complex contact experiences … and they carry the burden for their efforts.

These researchers often reside in a large international UFO community that basically adheres — in principle and in regards to the rules of engagement — to the traditional nuts-and-bolts North American school of Ufology, meaning they simply want recognition as serious scholars and, if and when possible, to be undisturbed by "outside" forces.

Unknown Down is clear in one of its underlying messages: Too many devoted and passionate researchers find themselves alone in this field and have no reason to keep up the good work out of fear and in light of several means of intimidation. The same holds true for sincere and well-intentioned eyewitnesses (both civilian and military). The more a UFO incident remains relevant and represents a problem for the national security of any nation, the more persuasive countermeasures are applied upon the witnesses and the researchers involved.

The witnesses of the events narrated and meticulously reconstructed in this book kept their mouths shut for long time. They knew what they saw weren't helicopters, or temperature inversions, or anything else that could be explained conventionally for that matter, and they most likely suffered for years in a state of psychological confusion, not knowing how or to whom to share their stories. With thousands of credible witnesses all over the world, it has become clear to me that no country offers their citizens a platform in which to speak their truth. Instead, governments create an atmosphere where witnesses, if they dare, talk at their own risk.

Take the case of the late Col. Philip J. Corso, who revealed in his book, *The Day After Roswell*, a great deal about the Pentagon's secret activities related to alien technology recovered from the Roswell, New Mexico, UFO crash. I remember when, during one of his two visits to Italy in 1997, I asked him a question about the danger of being a whistleblower. He replied, "Maurizio, I have received no threats, and I'm not afraid because they know the most important parts of the book are true. They can't change the facts. Roswell is history. After the incident and through significant back-engineering efforts, we achieved some results, but nothing of significance compared to what the ET's actually showed to us. For that we literally had to start from scratch with a new science."

History links *The Day After Roswell* and *Unknown Down* in several ways, which speaks to the frequency of UFO incidents and the patterns we see develop when we read about them. First is the issue of military personnel and their respect for national security, something Corso and Bill Schroeder adhered to during their service and for many years afterwards, even though they were compelled to share their stories immediately following their respective experiences. Corso used to say "no paper trail" was the motto of his intelligence network, referring to "verbal only" communication.

It is also no coincidence that Roth includes several other incidents involving the U.S. military in *Unknown Down.* He refers to the March 2, 1967, White Sands Missile Range incident "when two radars plotted 20 silver objects and radar blips at 7-mile altitude." A similar incident occurred 10 years earlier when Corso was stationed at White Sands and was responsible for radar operations. According to his military records, Corso was Battalion Commander from October 1957 to September 1958 in various Army Nike missile battery installations. At that time, White Sands was the largest military base in the United States and the nerve center of the Southwestern United States defense system. Corso wrote in both his book and his still-unpublished original notes (*Dawn of a New Age*) that on one hot day in the late summer of 1957, while he was inspecting the radar station connected to the White Sands range launching ramps, a radar man informed him an unknown blip appeared on the radars. The unit followed the object's track until it suddenly vanished from the screen.

Hypothetically, if one excludes a hyperspace jump, the reason for the disappearance could be either a crash impact or a crash landing. That's exactly what Corso thought in that moment, quickly figuring out the coordinates of the possible incident location in the high desert of New Mexico. He decided to follow his intuition and, having calculated the trajectory and the point of impact, Corso flew over the area on a small military plane with a young lieutenant pilot. When they reached the site, they saw "a shiny saucer-shaped object on the ground" that Corso interpreted as a missile booster. Two days later, Corso drove back to the site alone in his jeep. This led to a face-to-face encounter with an EBE (extraterrestrial biological entity) in the middle of the White Sands desert.

If the facts narrated by Corso are true (and I believe them to be based on my time spent with the man), flying saucers at that time, as well as in 1967, were quite vulnerable, at least at close range once detected by radar. They could malfunction and crash, and they could also be intercepted and shot down by one of our fighter jets. Based on what Bill Schroeder saw and heard on the night of March 31, 1967, as well as through his subsequent research, he came to the conclusion that the UFOs tracked on radar and seen over the skies of South Florida were actually searching for one of their own craft, and they weren't going to let some U.S. or Cuban fighter jets stop them!

After many years of UFO research, I've come to view the study of UFOs in North America as the most prolific in the world because, despite the risks, men and women from the U.S. military have come forward with their stories. Roth correctly credits individuals such as Robert Salas with being shining examples of why truth always trumps deception. The author also makes it a point to ask his readers to consider the risks these individuals take because they have little to no power relative to the U.S. military or government.

Roth's inclusion of several eyewitness accounts that end with the authorities either providing ridiculous explanations or, in the case of the military, stern warnings to remain silent, is frustrating and sobering because it implies that many researchers, witnesses and investigative journalists who normally wouldn't be afraid to search for the truth are discouraged from doing so because they receive push back from much more powerful and sinister forces. Yet the overall message of this book is a positive one, as it becomes clear to readers that, based on the credibility of the witnesses and sheer amount of corroborative, tangible evidence that has been accumulated over the years, UFOs are a real phenomenon and citizens of every country deserve to know the truth. People are sick and tired of the perennial state of secrecy and plausible denial put forth by their governments and demand more real evidence every day.

When I read this book, I thought about the late John Mack, the famous Harvard University psychiatrist who put his career at stake when he broached, studied and promoted the delicate question of human/alien abductions and extraterrestrial contacts. Without Mack's courage and tenacity, we would be still living in the dark when it comes to this important aspect of the UFO phenomenon.

The human factor plays a critical role in the never-ending chess game between ordinary citizens and the establishment, which includes mainstream scientific study, the military, the political class and dogma-laced Western religions. The overwhelming evidence suggests Earth has been visited by extraterrestrials for countless years, and yet the reality of these visitations in modern times has been stolen away and hidden from us. In *Unknown Down*, readers will find good investigative journalism combined with serious research and positive insight, a perfect elixir for readers who seek knowledge and demand the truth.

Introduction

When I first heard about the "incident over Miami," I was attending a StarworksUSA UFO symposium in Sebring, Fla. At the time, my colleagues and I were putting the finishing touches on our documentary film, "extraordinary: the stan romanek story," which endeavored to provide an objective account of one of the most documented, and controversial, alien abduction cases in the recorded history of this disturbing phenomenon. The project – a five-year, exhaustive journey filled with both frustrating challenges and satisfying successes – was transformational, as some of the experiences I had while making the film made me more convinced than ever that something very real and tangible was happening when it came to UFO encounters. As a result of these life-changing experiences, the possibility that extraterrestrials were visiting our planet, and in certain cases even interacting with humans, had become more than just plausible to me.

So, with an open mind and notepad in hand, I attended the Sebring symposium to continue to expand my knowledge on the UFO phenomenon and gain as much insight as possible from the impressive lineup of dedicated researchers and whistleblowers who were scheduled to speak that weekend. And with our documentary project almost complete, I was also hoping to find the next compelling story to share with the world.

As I meandered through the vendor area on the first day of the conference, I noticed a table with a stack of booklets on it. Having been raised in South Florida, I was intrigued by the title, "Incident Over Miami: A True UFO Story." Dennis Force, who was manning the table, greeted me with a smile and asked if I was having a good day.

"I am," I said. "Thank you for asking. What is this book about?"

"My cousin and I were both in the military in 1967 and were stationed in South Florida," began Dennis. "We had an incredible encounter with some UFOs one night, and this book recounts that story. It was a night neither of us has ever forgotten."

"Sounds really interesting," I responded. "I'd love to purchase one."

That night, I read the book, which was only about 30 pages long, and couldn't believe I had never before heard about this case in Ufology circles. According to the narrative, several "bogeys" were violating airspace in both the United States and Cuba during the height of the Cold War and only a few years removed from the Cuban Missile Crisis. Additionally, several U.S. missile bases, U.S. and Cuban military personnel, and numerous civilians were all either affected by or bore witness to the event. And perhaps most importantly, a Cuban fighter jet, sent to intercept the UFOs, was struck by some kind of electromagnetic pulse emitted from one of the unidentified craft. The fighter jet subsequently broke apart, killing the pilot.

The next morning I tracked down Dennis to learn more about the incident.

"Dennis, this story needs a bigger forum," I said. "Given the circumstances and the outcomes, this could be one of the most important UFO incidents never given the appropriate spotlight."

"I agree wholeheartedly," he responded. "I'll put you in touch with my cousin Bill, who was stationed in Key West when this happened. He's the one who put this research together. He's been looking into this case for years and can give you more insight."

"Definitely," I thanked him. "I'd love to talk to Bill about making this a full-blown book. The story most definitely warrants it."

Dennis told me more about what he experienced from his perspective, and we both agreed that the story needed to be shared with as many people as possible. As an ex-military man bound by duty, he never really spoke with anyone about the incident except for Bill, who had always been like a brother to him. Having felt forced to live with a pretty big secret for years, Dennis was now on board with making this story available for public consumption.

Weeks later, when I finally spoke with Bill Schroeder, I found him to be both affable and sincere. These initial discussions stirred me further, as I felt both Bill and Dennis struggled with the secrecy surrounding the incident and were determined to get the entire story out there. At this point in his life, Bill was dedicated to finding out as much as he could from other witnesses, and I wanted to help him by sharing his story and framing it in the larger context of Ufology. I told Bill this was one of those stories that compels us to ask the big-picture questions associated with UFO encounters and the secrecy surrounding them. This would provide an opportunity to offer additional insight to readers.

Why did several unidentified objects, flying at speeds superior to our capabilities and performing aerial maneuvers beyond our known laws of physics, conduct what seemed to be a grid search over South Florida and the Atlantic Ocean on March 31, 1967?

Why did the military attempt to cover up the incident by telling their personnel that it was nothing more than a NORAD exercise and that they were never to talk about it with anyone?

How did these UFOs manage to render ineffective all of the high-tech electronics in a missile battery and on a Cuban fighter jet?

What is the significance of tracking UFOs on radar when it comes to producing tangible evidence of their existence?

What is the significance of UFO encounters on U.S. missile bases?

We may never find the answers to any of these questions, but, as a storyteller, I feel obligated to share the stories that spark these questions with all of humanity. There are many individuals like Bill and Dennis, both military and civilian, whose lives have been adversely affected because of something they saw in the sky, tracked on radar or physically encountered on the ground. We owe it to them to doggedly seek out the truth, no matter how uncomfortable it makes those who would prefer us live like lemmings, never questioning the true reality of the world, and the universe, in which we live.

I'm grateful Bill agreed to have me write his story, as he has definitely been motivated to find even a modicum of closure regarding that night of March 31, 1967. As a man of action and principle, he also wants to validate his experience and let other military personnel who have had similar experiences know they are not alone. Whether these men and women were sitting behind radar screens, piloting aircraft or ordered to cover up evidence when these UFO incidents took place, Bill wants to help them by coming forward publicly with his story. If this book helps one or two – or hopefully 100 or 1,000 – people understand the importance of sharing their stories, we all benefit.

While this incident may have occurred decades ago, the fact it was kept quiet doesn't make it any less relevant. As a journalist, I feel compelled to investigate the possibility that a perceived truth may not be the truth at all, but instead a lie intended to "protect" the masses. Just because something is deemed a NORAD exercise, or swamp gas, or a hallucination doesn't necessarily make it so, especially when logic and common sense suggest otherwise and significant effort is brought to bear by powerful entities in order to maintain secrecy.

In many ways, this story is just beginning because a new generation is hearing about it for the first time. The goal of this book is to encourage readers, both young and old, to question tired paradigms and open up to new possibilities … and wonder … and ask more questions … and learn … and learn some more … and understand … and evolve.

Chapter One

The World Stage in 1967

The 1960s was a decade of turmoil, and much has been written about the unrest caused as a result of the John. F. Kennedy assassination, the Vietnam War, the Civil Rights Movement, and the assassinations of Martin Luther King and Bobby Kennedy. It also had its high points, as The Beatles revolutionized music around the world and Neil Armstrong became the first human being to step foot on the moon.

1967 was a particularly turbulent year, as the continued presence of American troops in Vietnam increased further, bringing the total to 475,000 U.S. soldiers serving in Southeast Asia. Peace rallies grew and intensified as the number of people disillusioned by U.S. foreign policy grew. Major race riots took place in Newark and Detroit. Sports icon Muhammad Ali was stripped of his boxing title for refusing to be inducted into the U.S.

Army. In the Middle East, Israel went to war with Syria, Egypt and Jordan in what became known as the Six-Day War; and when it was over, Israel seized control of the Gaza Strip and the Sinai Peninsula from Egypt, the West Bank and East Jerusalem from Jordan, and the Golan Heights from Syria.

During the summer months, cities throughout the United States exploded in rioting and looting, the worst being in Detroit, where 7,000 National Guards were brought in to restore law and order on the streets. A deep-seeded mistrust of America's oldest institutions continued to grow among the younger generations. The hippie counterculture was in full bloom, as the Summer of Love saw 100,000 people converge in the Haight-Ashbury neighborhood of San Francisco and thousands more pour into other major cities across the United States. For a time, these cities became melting pots of politics, music, drugs, creativity and the total lack of sexual and social inhibition.

In addition to everything else, 1967 occurred during the height of the Cold War. Along with an escalating war in Vietnam, the United States and its allies were fighting a global political battle against powers in the Eastern Bloc (the Soviet Union and its allies in the Warsaw Pact). Holding the line against communist threats and aggression all over the world, the U.S. government's biggest concern was the possibility of a nuclear first strike against its own homeland. The Cuban Missile Crisis of 1962 successfully brought to the forefront of the American psyche just how close the United States came to a catastrophic nuclear holocaust. South Floridians, in particular, were very well aware how close they were to enemy weapons of mass destruction.

South Florida was the location of many important events during the Cold War. The region served as a forward command center for the projection of U.S. power into the Western Hemisphere throughout the conflict. The region's proximity to Latin America made it an operational center for both covert and overt activities as the United States pursued its policy of containing communism. From the 1950s to the end of the Cold War in 1989, government officials directed operations from South Florida military installations such as Homestead Air Force Base, Opa Locka Marine Air Station, and the various U.S. Navy facilities in Key West that affected events in Guatemala, Cuba, Nicaragua and other nations throughout Latin America.

From Miami to Key West, quiet residential neighborhoods were havens for undercover operatives while swamps and forests served as training grounds. The United States launched numerous operations from South Florida, including the overthrow of the Arbenz government in Guatemala in 1954; the unsuccessful Bay of Pigs invasion of 1961; the military buildup necessitated by the Cuban Missile Crisis of 1962; surveillance, intelligence and espionage activities against Cuba, Nicaragua, and other nations; and radio and television propaganda broadcasting to Cuba. All of these activities were justified under the U.S. foreign policy of containment. As the South Florida region helped shape these events, the events would impact South Florida's society, culture, demographics, and history in ways deemed unimaginable before the Cold War.

When the establishment of Soviet missile bases in Cuba in 1962 became a serious threat to national security, U.S. defense officials implemented military contingency plans. They began a massive military alert in the United States, and all sorts of personnel, money, and military equipment flooded into South Florida and bases such as Homestead AFB, Key West National Air Station and Naval Station, Opa Locka Airport, Port Everglades and other facilities. The United States was prepared to go to war over the issue of nuclear missiles in Cuba. And if necessary, the island would be invaded with all the might of the U.S. military.

Defense planners and intelligence analysts never really believed that a credible threat to national security could emanate from anywhere in the Western Hemisphere. The Cuban Missile Crisis changed that type of thinking, and military officials scrambled to tighten up the U.S. air defense perimeter. In order to defend against the possibility of an air attack on Miami and the region's strategic military staging areas, the Army deployed several air defense missile battalions to the region. Both HAWK (Homing All the Way Killer) and Nike Hercules missile battalions arrived in South Florida within days of the onset of the crisis. Missile batteries were installed throughout South Florida and in Key West. While the massive buildup was only temporary and the crisis was eventually averted, the deployment resulted in the permanent establishment of an all-altitude, anti-aircraft missile defense system designed to counter the threat of both Soviet and Cuban air attacks.

Troops in South Florida served in a unique capacity within Army Air Defense Command by virtue of the fact that the threat of attack was often much more real than that faced by other batteries across the United States. They operated the only defense integrating HAWK and Nike batteries and fulfilled unique mobility requirements given to no other stateside Nike batteries. South Florida troops also had a unique complement of weapons, including the Anti-Tactical Ballistic Missile version of the Hercules that could shoot down tactical ballistic missiles. They could use their missiles and their mobility to fulfill a surface-to-surface mission if necessary, which meant they could strike targets on the ground and in the air.

The military men and women who were stationed in South Florida in 1967 were well trained and well armed, but nothing could prepare them for what happened on the night of March 31.

Chapter Two

"The Night"

During the heart of the Cold War, the nation depended on NORAD (North American Air Defense Command) to protect it from sneak attack. NORAD was formed in September 1957 following an agreement between the governments of Canada and the United States that officially recognized the fact that the air defense of the two countries had to be a united task. A high-level Canadian-United States committee (Military Cooperation Committee) drew up an emergency plan for the common defense of North America and directed the air defense organizations of the two countries to develop a detailed emergency air defense plan. NORAD was born from that directive.

Located deep within the Colorado Rockies mountain range, NORAD's underground headquarters represents the most sophisticated air defense system in the world. The men and women who are stationed at NORAD monitor the skies of the Western Hemisphere for potential threats against North America. In 1967, the eyes and ears of NORAD were the hundreds of radar stations dotting the national landscape and operated by all branches of the U.S. military. These radar installations stretched from the Canadian Polar regions to the southernmost tips of the United States.

"The Night" refers to an extraordinary event that occurred on the night of March 31, 1967, involving two of these radar stations. Although the action that night centered in South Florida, it actually started much farther to the north. At approximately 10:30 p.m., both Canadian and U.S. air defense units began to track eight unidentified targets moving from north to south along the Atlantic coast. The targets, which were moving at incredible speeds, originated from the North Pole region. They were immediately tagged as unidentified potentially hostile targets – or bogeys in military lingo – as they proceeded down the coast.

***

Air Force communications specialist Dennis Force was passing the night away at his radar post near Homestead Air Force Base. Attempting to liven up an otherwise boring evening, he was chatting on a three-way communications line with several local nursing students and his cousin, Bill Schroeder, a fire control operator at B Battery in Key West. Dennis was surprised when he received an incoming bogey alert to the 644th Radar Squadron. As military business always came before pleasure, he said a quick goodnight to his nurse friends and put his cousin on hold.

Bill Schroeder
Army 1967

Dennis Force
USAF 1967

The alert was an advisory to the 644th that a number of bogeys were heading towards the Miami area. At the time, Force had no idea what these bogeys could be, but he quickly alerted the others on duty and walked a few feet away to a radarscope manned by one of his fellow airmen. They were stunned by what they saw. The targets entered the area from the north at speeds that were simply unattainable by any military aircraft they knew of. The experienced operators were told these objects were tracked for over an hour at speeds ranging from 1,600 mph to their current speed of nearly 5,000 mph. The bogeys, in a tight formation, suddenly decelerated as they entered the skies just east of Miami.

The airmen knew this was no malfunction. Nor was it a temperature inversion or other type of anomaly. It was a clear, cold night, and these were solid objects executing turns and maneuvers as a unified group. Clearly these were some type of aircraft moving under intelligent control. Whoever, or whatever, they were, they were violating U.S. airspace and needed to be dealt with.

Approximately 120 miles to the south, Bill Schroeder was waiting on hold for his cousin to get back on the phone. He was also trying to pass another boring night of standby duty at his HAWK missile battery. It could get pretty lonely in the Battery Control Center. Day or night, it was always dark, and the various colored, glowing panel lights made it seem like you were in the interior of a starship. It was another 15 minutes before Force came back on the line, and his tone changed. Gone was the laissez-faire, flirting-with-the-nurses attitude. His voice bellowed with a sense of urgency.

"You can't believe what's happening here, Bill. It's UFOs, real UFOs!" Dennis exclaimed into the telephone.

At first, Schroeder did not believe what he was hearing, and he half expected his cousin to crack up laughing at any moment. The two grew up together like brothers, and there was no end to the practical jokes they played on each other over the years. They joined two separate branches of the service one year apart, and by

B Battery Control Center Interior

amazing coincidence, they ended up stationed in their home state less than a two-hour car ride apart.

"I'll let you listen in, but don't say anything," Force cautioned.

With a flip of the switch at Homestead, Schroeder was now eavesdropping on various air defense radar and command stations across the protective net. The chatter was devoted to the bogeys cruising the skies off the Florida coast. Schroeder was able to monitor the traffic for a few minutes before he was cut off again. One thing became perfectly clear to him ... this was no practical joke between cousins.

Force was working hard to keep the communication lines open while watching the incredible sight being displayed on the scopes of the 644th. They were tracking eight targets flying in two separate groups. The farthest group was 60 to 80 miles out in the Atlantic Ocean. The nearest group was just 3 to 4 miles off the coast of Homestead and well south of Miami.

Overcome by curiosity, Schroeder was in the process of bringing up his Key West pulse acquisition radar, or PAR, from standby to active mode when his cousin called back.

"Everyone here is crapping in their pants," Force said. "These things are zipping around at impossible speeds."

Schroeder was still bringing up his electronics as he listened to Force's excitement. "Any word from NORAD?" he asked.

"Heck no. They're flabbergasted," Force replied. "They don't have a clue what these things are."

At that moment, the radar monitor on Schroeder's fire control console lit up, the green sweep line circling the scope, and the track matching the movement of the large antenna some 80 feet above his head.

The targets came into view at the top of the scope, looking like green tadpoles as they crossed the screen. "I've got them. Holy crap, I really got them! I've got three … no four … four solid targets moving east to west in line formation at maximum range," Schroeder told Force. "Judas Priest, these suckers are hauling ass! Definitely supersonic!"

"We've got eight bogeys here, Bill, in two groups," said Force, who was still tracking the objects with his fellow airmen. "The four to the north must be beyond your horizon."

"My targets are clearly flying a grid, east to west and north to south," Schroeder reported back.

"We agree, Bill. It looks like a search pattern," Force replied. "They're doing a complete overfly of the Atlantic coast from Fort Lauderdale to south of Homestead. The four to the north are staying far out over the Atlantic."

Out on the missile launch pad of B Battery in Key West, the launch crew chief and his three missile technicians were silently alerted to unexpected activity when the pulse acquisition radar came online and started spinning. The experienced crew chief immediately began preflight checks on his birds and launchers. He knew if the PAR was brought on line this time of night, a "hot status alert" was only moments away, and he was not waiting for an engraved invitation to get his station ready. It was his job to ensure his birds would be ready to fly at a moment's notice if needed.

It was now an hour since these strange objects first arrived in the Miami area, and Schroeder was no longer amused by the spectacle being displayed on the scope in front of him. Deep in his heart, he knew he was witness to something amazing and that these moments would change his life forever. He knew instinctively these bogeys could not be Russian, or anything else manmade for that matter. No aircraft in 1967 could even come close to those speeds, and no pilot could ever survive the sudden and sharp turns these craft were making with incredible acceleration.

As he contemplated what these objects could be and who or what could be flying them, three more targets suddenly appeared on the scope. They were coming from Boca Chica Naval Air Station, which was a couple of miles north of his battery. Heading north towards Miami at supersonic speed, they were U.S. Navy Phantom fighter jets on their way to check out the bogeys in Miami.

Still on the secure phone line with his cousin, Schroeder relayed the news. "We're going to know who they are in a few minutes, Denny. I'm tracking three friendly fast-movers heading your way," said Schroeder, referring to the supersonic Navy aircraft.

Schroeder tracked the Navy Phantoms advancing up the coast towards the intruders, who continued to fly the same pattern off the coast of Miami. His eyes focused intently on the radar screen, and then he watched in disbelief as the physically impossible happened. As the U.S. fighters closed in to about 40 miles from the bogeys, the unknowns disappeared off the scope.

"Dennis, they're gone!" he exclaimed into the phone. "It's not possible, but it just happened."

"Gone here, too, Bill," Force replied. "That's freaking unbelievable. No lateral acceleration. They just vanished."

"There's only one way they could do that, Denny," Schroeder said. "They either had to travel straight up or straight down."

For 15 minutes, the intercepting fighters cruised the skies over the Atlantic coast before turning south towards Key West and back to their base. At the radar sites in Homestead and Key West, the operators watched as the Phantoms, by now likely low on fuel, headed back. And then, as the Navy fighters crossed the halfway point between Miami and Key West, the bogeys suddenly returned to the scopes.

First moving in a close formation, the bogeys fanned out into two groups and resumed the same square flight pattern. It was evident by the radio traffic that NORAD was now in panic mode. Unknown aircraft were flying through American airspace with impunity. Nobody had any idea who they were, where they came from, or what their intentions were. And, if the Soviet Union did have that kind of technology, the Cold War would be over sooner rather than later, and Americans would be learning to speak Russian.

Just after midnight, U.S. Air Force intercept jets arrived in the area only to find what the Phantom jets had earlier. As before, as soon as the fighters left the area, the strange visitors returned.

Whoever they were, they were determined to complete their mission, whatever that was.

As the early morning hours approached, the bogeys continued to fly the same square grid pattern they were flying since their arrival over Miami. It was clear these bogeys were looking for something or someone in the Atlantic Ocean off the Florida coast.

"I just realized something, Dennis," Schroeder said. "These turkeys are in the Bermuda Triangle."

Force laughed. "Yeah, the science fiction writers will have a ball with this one."

The time passed, and the cat-and-mouse game continued. As Schroeder watched his scope in Key West, something had changed. One target was breaking formation with a lateral move. The lone bogey was heading south directly towards Key West. He estimated the object's speed at 1,600 mph.

Force noticed the activity as well. "One target headed your way, cuz!" he quipped.

Schroeder quickly brought up additional radar units and tracking gear. "I got him, Denny," he said. "He's gonna be in my playground in a minute." Then, speaking softly to himself, he said, "I've got you now sucker, just keep coming south."

Out in the launch area, the crew chief watched the radar towers with a keen eye. When the targeting radar came online and swung around to the north, he knew his battery was definitely tracking something. He quickly finished his preflight checks on the fighters and led his crew off the launch pads to the safety of the J Box, a small shed located a secure distance from the launchers that kept them from getting fried to a crisp when the fighters took flight.

Inside the Battery Control Center, two things became very clear to Schroeder. He had a target 60 miles away doing about 25 miles a minute, and he only had a few seconds to bring the additional electronics to bear. Force was still in his headset, but he had to focus on the bogey. Schroeder, an experienced fire control operator, was on autopilot. One hand was on the azimuth control knob to point the targeting radar, while the other adjusted the PAR and illuminator systems to maintain a crisp target return.

He also switched his headset input from communicating with Force to radar Doppler. Listening to the Doppler shift allowed radar operators to actually hear the radar signal transmissions reflected by a target. Experienced operators were able to distinguish some aircraft types and determine if a target was inbound or outbound. At this moment, Schroeder smiled as he remembered a drive-in movie from long ago and again quietly spoke to himself. “This is *Earth Battles the UFOs* … for real.”

The lone bogey was now 25 miles away when he locked on with the targeting radar. The Doppler return was heard clearly, a high-pitched whine he had never heard before, not from any radar target. A solid lock would allow accurate speed and altitude tracking. Schroeder was pleased with his success.

“Got ya, sucker,” he said to no one in particular.

Unfortunately, his exuberance was short-lived. The lock lasted about five seconds before all hell broke loose. The radar sweeps flashed, stopped and then reversed direction before blacking out completely. The control center, which was brightly lit and alive with sensor lights and illuminated switches just moments before, was now a dark cave. He immediately knew he was hit with some type of electronic countermeasure, or ECM. There was no doubt whoever or whatever was flying that craft reacted to the lock-on and responded by disabling the missile site.

ECM is a type of electronic warfare involving actions taken to prevent or reduce the effectiveness of enemy equipment and tactics that employ or are affected by electromagnetic radiations. By 1967, the United States Air Force aircraft were equipped with varying types of intercept receivers, transmitting electronic jammers and chaff dispensers contingent upon the tactics to be employed. Intelligence reports indicated potential enemies of the United States had spent vast amounts of money in development of ECM equipment.

From a tactical standpoint, ECM is introduced into a radar receiver to impair the use of the reflected radar signal. If a jamming signal enters the receiver and prevents the radar operator from seeing the target or causes the operator to lose the target, the jamming has reduced the effectiveness of the air defense. The susceptibility of radar equipment to jamming forced military planners to come up with extensive improvements to radar systems that allowed effective operation despite heavy jamming.

These electronic counter-countermeasures (ECCM) were already in existence and operating within NORAD's radar stations in 1967. The fact that someone, or something, could render an entire HAWK missile battery nonoperational was astounding, unheard of and scary as hell, especially in South Florida just a few years removed from the Cuban Missile Crisis.

The launch crew chief and his technicians were intently looking north in an effort to determine what was being tracked when the entire site went black. Off in the distant sky, a new light source came into view. A white ball of light was closing in on the missile site at lightning-fast speed. B Battery was briefly illuminated as the light passed over north to south and disappeared over the horizon. The launch chief ran the short distance to the control center just as a very confused Schroeder exited.

"We saw it, Bill. That thing was hauling ass," he said. "It looked like a meteorite, but it was in level flight."

"That was no meteor," Schroeder responded. " I've been tracking him and his buddies all night."

The launch chief gazed back at him with a puzzled look: "Did you say 'buddies'?"

In Miami, Force was unaware of the happenings in Key West. He knew his cousin had locked on a single bogey, and then all contact was lost. His attempts to reconnect were unsuccessful. The remaining targets accelerated to the east out over the Atlantic and soon disappeared.

The UFOs were gone, leaving behind a great mystery. Over the years, Schroeder and Force would refer to this incident as "the night." Today, almost 50 years later, "the night" still haunts them, and many unanswered questions still remain.

B Battery Key West Today

Chapter Three

Cuba Gets Involved

At the same time U.S. air defense units in South Florida were scrambling to get a handle on the unknown bogeys, two Cuban Air Force MiG-21s were on routine combat air patrol along the northern Cuban coast. The Mikoyan-Gurevich MiG-21 was a supersonic jet fighter aircraft designed by the Mikoyan-Gurevich Design Bureau in the Soviet Union. It was the first successful Soviet aircraft combining fighter and interceptor characteristics in a single aircraft. The MiG-21 was the standard, top-of-the-line fighter jet supplied to Soviet bloc countries and was one of the most prolific aircraft of the Cold War. The two fighter jets were armed with four K-13 air-to-air missiles and cannons. After liftoff, they climbed slowly to their patrol altitude of 15,000 feet.

The patrol was fairly mundane, that is until the commanding pilot's radio came to life. Cuban air defense radar stations were tracking an unknown target entering Cuban air space at high speed (nearly 660 mph) and at a height of about 33,000 feet. The target track had initiated in the United States, which led the commanding pilot to believe it was another American aerial reconnaissance flight making sure Russian missiles were not sitting in a Cuban battery somewhere, poised to launch at the United States.

Spanish-speaking intercept operators of the 6947th Security Squadron Detachment A, located at Key West Naval Air Station, heard the entire communications between Cuban ground control intercept radar personnel and the two MiG pilots that night. The series of events, in summation, are as follows:

Given the vector to an interception point, the commander and his wingman turned their aircraft and throttled up. Now at supersonic speeds, they were closing in on the unknown target at 19,000 feet. The commander radioed that the object was a bright metallic spheroid disc with no visible markings or appendages. When a try at radio contact failed, Cuban air defense headquarters ordered him to arm his weapons and destroy the object. His headset crackled with the sound of his command, "Vibora 1, you are cleared to fire."

As he locked on his target, he transmitted to his wingman:

"Vibora 1 to Vibora 2, I have target lock ….."

The wingman was listening to the partial transmission when a brilliant flash of light blinded him. When the air cleared and his vision returned, he was stunned to see his commander was gone.

His MiG-21 was now a stream of fast-moving debris traveling in a long arc through the night sky towards the ground.

The commander's fighter disintegrated. The electronic countermeasure that had crippled the missile battery in Key West apparently had the same effect on the MiG. With its electronics and avionics systems rendered useless, the aircraft simply came apart in flight.

The wingman screamed to the ground controller that his leader's jet exploded: "Vibora 1 is gone. I repeat, Vibora 1 is gone!"

When he regained his composure, he radioed that there was no smoke or flame, and that his leader's MiG-21 disintegrated in midair.

The wingman, eager to avenge the death of his friend, prepared to engage the bogey as it climbed away and accelerated. Cuban command, however, did not want to lose another aircraft. Realizing further pursuit was dangerous, and most likely useless, the Cuban fighter control ordered him to disengage.

"Vibora 2, return to base immediately."

At last report, the UFO was heading south-southwest towards South America.

As the stunned pilot turned for home, he wondered about the strange craft. Could it be American? No. Not possible. But then who?

The 6947th Security Squadron sent an Intelligence Spot Report to National Security Agency (NSA) headquarters. Such reports are standard practice in cases of aircraft losses by hostile nations. The NSA is required to acknowledge receipt of such reports, but the

6947th did not get one, so it sent a follow-up report. Within hours, personnel of Detachment A received orders to ship all tapes and pertinent data to the NSA and to list the Cuban aircraft loss in squadron files as "due to equipment malfunction." At least 15 to 20 individuals in the detachment were fully informed of the incident. Presumably, the data sent to the NSA included direction-finding measurements that the agency might later combine with other site data to triangulate the location and altitude of the MiG-21 flight paths. If the equipment in Florida was sensitive enough, the UFO could have been tracked by its reflection off the Cuban ground and airborne radar.

In their book, *Clear Intent: The Government Coverup of the UFO Experience*, National Investigations Committee on Aerial Phenomena (NICAP) researchers Barry Greenwood and Lawrence Fawcett talk about an amazing development surrounding the 1967 Cuban MiG incident that emphasized the strong national security nature of the UFO phenomenon.

Apparently, Citizens Against UFO Secrecy (CAUS) became aware of the incident in the form of a statement by a security specialist who was assigned to the 6947th Security Squadron (Detachment A) located at Homestead Air Force Base. The specialist attended a lecture in 1978 by nuclear physicist and UFO researcher Stanton Friedman, and he informed Friedman of the incident at the conclusion of the talk. Friedman asked for additional details, which were provided later in the form of a typed statement by the specialist.

Friedman sent the statement to Robert Pratt, a reporter who worked for the National Enquirer. Pratt, in turn, sent the statement to Robert Todd, CAUS Research Director, desiring to verify the accuracy of the story. Todd began to look into it.

Due to the story's direct relevance to this case, here is what happened to Todd as told in its entirety by Greenwood and Fawcett:

> *Todd sent information requests concerning the Cuban incident to the Air Force, CIA, NSA and the Navy between February and July of 1978, all without success. On March 10, the CIA and suggested that Todd check within the Cuban government for records on the incident. Todd notified both the NSA and the Air Force on July 14 that because neither agency wished to cooperate, he would contact the Cuban government for further information. Since he thought both agencies hinted that he might have classified data, Todd asked that they provide advice as to what information in the attached statement should not be transmitted to the Cubans. Todd gave them a 20-day deadline for replies, but he did not have to wait long.*
>
> *On July 28, 1978, between 5:30 and 6 p.m., Todd's mother answered a knock at the door. Two men, one older than the other, asked for Todd. When Todd came downstairs, one of the men asked if he was Robert Todd. He replied "yes." The men then flashed their identification cards. Todd knew what it was about as soon as he saw "FBI." Todd and the two agents went into the living room, while Todd's parents kept their St. Bernard dog occupied*

outside. The two men read Todd his rights and then asked him to sign a paper that said this they had done so. Todd waived his right to silence because he felt that he did not have anything to hide. One of the men began to read the espionage laws, but Todd told them that he was already familiar with them. They told Todd that the laws carry a penalty of life in prison or death. Both agents hinted at the possibility some indictments would be issued.

Todd, who earlier advised the NSA and the Air Force he might write to Cuba for details of the violent MiG-21 encounter with the UFO, said the agents asked him if he had ever written to a foreign government. Todd said that he had written to the Soviet Union, but explained that it was an innocent query. The older FBI agent told Todd that the Bureau had been asked by the NSA to investigate this matter because the NSA has no law enforcement functions.

The two agents sat on opposite sides of him as they conducted the interview. Todd told us that he felt like a Ping Pong ball. One of them took the hard line and the other took the soft line. They indicated that they knew or had copies of Todd's July 14 letter to the NSA with the attached security specialist's letter. They asked Todd to identify the source of the letter. Todd told them a researcher (Friedman) had obtained the statement and passed it on to a reporter, who, in turn, passed it on to Todd. The question was asked several times because the younger agent kept confusing the "researcher" with the "reporter." Todd eventually identified. They next pressed

Todd about the researcher, and when Todd refused to identify him, the agents pressed him to reveal if he was on the East or West coast. Todd told them the West coast. One agent asked Todd if information in the source's statement was ever published. Todd said that it had not been published to his knowledge. At the time, he did not know that Friedman had released the story to UPI.

Todd was not without some questions of his own; he wanted to know if any information in the source's statement was classified and at what level. The older agent, described by Todd as having a granite face and wearing a white suit, replied, "Some of the information is classified. Most of it is bullshit."

The question of tapping Todd's phone arose. At one point, Todd told the agents that based on the information they had given him, it seemed they had sufficient justification for a wiretap on his telephone. They both smiled.

Todd told both agents that under the authority of the Freedom of Information Act, he was going to demand the FBI file on its investigation of him. Surprisingly, they said they couldn't send the information that Todd had just given them because it was classified! Todd told them, "I have read enough FBI documents to know they always refer to the subject by saying 'captioned as above.'" He wanted to know how they were going to caption this one: "Internal Security" or "Espionage"? One of the agents replied that it was neither; it would fall under "Counterespionage."

When the two agents were leaving, they met Todd's parents, who had been in the dining room during the last half-hour of the session. Todd's mother asked if her son was in trouble. One of the agents said, no, that Todd was the "man on the end of the string." In recounting the incident, Todd said that the agent said it straight-faced, and he thought he meant every word. His mother told him, "You ought to get the top guy." A bemused Todd thought, "She was a big help."

Todd informed CAUS that he had been visited by the agents, so CAUS contacted Paul B. Lorenzetti, spokesman for the FBI field division in Philadelphia, on July 31. When questioned about the Todd visit by agents of the FBI, Lorenzetti stated, "I'm not aware of anything about the Todd investigation," but he added, "I'm not cleared to gain information in such investigations. I have very little contact with the security end of everything." Pressed for more information, Lorenzetti reiterated, "I just don't have any knowledge of any of this," and he suggested a "call back later after I have got security to look into it." On August 1, CAUS again called Lorenzetti, who put special agent Roger Midkiff on the line, but first explained, "I've already given him instructions, if there is a pending investigation, he is not to make any comments. That is the official policy of the Bureau, as far the Attorney General's guidelines are concerned."

Agent Midkiff said that if there was an investigation, there might be some official statement on it when it was complete. CAUS also called FBI headquarters in Washington, D.C., and talked to spokesman John Perks, who stated that he, too, knew nothing about an investigation of Todd. "I don't have any knowledge of this; we're going to have to check," he said. Later that day, Perk's superior, Tom Coll, called CAUS and said, "We never confirm who we've talked to or who we haven't talked to. We never do that." Coll said near the end of his call, "Whether we have had agents talk to him or we haven't, I don't know. But even if I did, we wouldn't confirm or deny it."

CAUS called the NSA at its headquarters in central Maryland and talked to Charles Sullivan, spokesman for the NSA. Sullivan stated, "If the way for the NSA to salvage the situation was to use what we will call the 'ways and means' technique of reducing the impact; that is, the incident is unimportant, but the methods of receipt are classified.

Todd filed a request with the Air Force to obtain copies of his FOIA case file on the matter (all documents generated as a result of his requests). The executive officer of the USAF's Office of the Judge Advocate General, Col. James Johnson, replied in a September 14 letter, stating:

"You have requested information of the classification of the 'statement' attached to your letter of 14 July 1978 addressed to Mr. Nelson. You are advised that the Air Force can neither confirm nor deny the authenticity of this statement, nor the existence of any records concerning the incident described therein [emphasis

added]. However, if authentic, I am advised the statement would be classified Secret in its entirety."

Col. Johnson advised Todd that he could only have letters that Todd had sent and received, excluding the "security analyst's" statement, which Todd had anyway. Johnson finally proceeded to describe 10 documents that related to Todd's request and were classified under the national security provisions of the FOIA.

These events, as described, clearly indicate that the Cuban incident was most probably authentic, that Robert Todd and CAUS were on to a big story, and that the government experienced a knee-jerk reaction to the fact that the story got out. Todd honestly tried to follow up the original story as any intelligent person would when have such a story virtually dropped into his lap. The inquiries were structured specifically to spare the government undue embarrassment. Yet the reaction was to "sic" the FBI on Todd with the purpose of scaring him out of his wits. Such tactics do not work well in a democratic society, and whoever decided to take this course was ill advised. The story remains a baffling mystery, and one wonders how many more of those incidents lie in state in the NSA's files, among others.

Over time, many elements of the 1967 incident over South Florida have been pieced together slowly. Years after Greenwood and Fawcett wrote about the Cuban MiG incident and Robert Todd's experiences with the FBI, Schroeder retired and finally felt comfortable coming forward with his own experiences regarding "the night," and he eventually called Stanton Friedman to tell him what he and his cousin witnessed. Their experiences, as well as those of the other eyewitnesses mentioned in this book, represent the kind of corroborative evidence that makes UFO cases so compelling.

At the time of the incident, Schroeder and Force knew nothing about the Cuban MiG pilots, but as more and more people started to talk about what happened, each testimony began to support the other, creating a more complete picture of what transpired not only on the night of March 31, but in the subsequent weeks and months that followed.

Chapter Four

Aftermath

As daylight broke the following morning, Force and the other men of the 644th were already being debriefed. A major they had never seen before, accompanied by two clean-cut, serious-looking men in dark suits, spoke to the exhausted airmen and their commanding officer.

"What you saw last night was a NORAD exercise, nothing more," cautioned the Major. "You're not to talk about it with anyone."

Force admitted feeling intimidated. "We had never seen these men before, so for them to debrief us the way they did, and by basically offering no plausible explanation whatsoever regarding the previous night's events, it was more than a bit unnerving to be standing in front of these guys, especially the two men in suits."

Having a top-secret clearance, Force took to heart what his superior said about not talking to anyone about the incident. If he did open his mouth, he could wind up in Leavenworth Federal Prison Camp, or even worse based on the way these hard-looking men were conducting themselves. It seemed to Force they were trained to act this way for maximum effect, and it worked.

The men of the 644th just stood there and looked at each other in disbelief. They knew the Major was lying, but they could not figure out why. While the Major spoke, the two men in dark suits began to confiscate the visual recordings of the radar activity from the previous evening. They secured all the evidence in a very workmanlike manner.

"They took everything we had," said Force. "In those days, we had tape-to-tape video reels of our radar screens. They took those, all of our paperwork ... everything that had anything to do with the incident was taken from our possession in short order."

Within a few minutes, the Major and his dark-suited cohorts were gone, and so was all the evidence. To the members of the 644th, the whole debriefing felt both surreal and off-putting.

Force remembers feeling both confused and angry by the way it all went down. He and his colleagues knew that this Major, whoever he was, was lying to them. "The thought that what we had just witnessed was a NORAD exercise was absurd," he explained. "It was obviously a cover up, but at the time we were basically kids and terrified of these guys, so I never talked about the incident with anyone, except for Bill, until many years later when I was out of the military and retired."

In Key West, a similar scene was playing out. Schroeder's superiors told him and his fellow battery mates the entire episode was simply a NORAD military exercise and that nothing was what it appeared to be so they should forget the whole thing. They also told them the incident was not classified, but it was still a forbidden topic of conversation. At first, he could not understand what they meant, but then it dawned on him. The mere act of classifying the incident would verify its occurrence, which was the last thing "they" wanted.

"They basically made it a non-issue," explained Schroeder. "Looking back, it was a really clever way to handle the situation, but I was also extremely agitated by that and knew they were full of it. That feeling has never left me. I just put it away as one of those things I knew to be true but that the military would never admit to."

When Schroeder and Force next spoke to each other, there was little said about what would become known between them as "the night." Within three months, most of the crewmen who shared the experience received transfer orders. Force was sent to Melville Air Force Base in Labrodor, Goose Bay, Newfoundland, as an armed forces radio DJ. His commanding officer was sent to Europe. Schroeder was ordered to Korea and transferred to the military police. Neither Force nor Schroeder would ever sit in front of a radar monitor again.

"Goose Bay is a very remote site," said Force. "I was there for an entire year, and I always believed they were trying to stop us from talking by separating the witnesses. They actually sent the duty officer who was in charge that night along with me to Goose

Bay, so they did a good job of making sure we both wound up in the middle of nowhere, at least for a while."

For Schroeder, being transferred to Korea as a military policeman always struck him as strange. "It seemed like they wanted to separate the witnesses and send us off to various locations around the world," he said. "Transfers are part of military service, and you learn to get used to them, but the fact that just about everyone involved in the unexplained events of that evening were transferred as far away from each other as possible is too much of a coincidence, especially after having been told it was a 'non-event' and a 'forbidden topic of conversation.'"

Over the years, from time to time, Schroeder and Force would talk about "the night." They shared the incident and their involvement only with each other and close family members. Both men understood, having chosen careers in public service, they could never go public with their story without risking severe damage to their careers and reputations. After his military service, Force became a white-collar crime investigator for the State of Florida. Schroeder had a long career as a police officer and retired as a major crimes investigator. It wasn't until 35 years after the incident, once they had both retired from public service, that they were comfortable going public with their story.

Chapter Five

Other Eyewitnesses

Outside the secure military bases where Schroeder and Force were tracking these mysterious bogeys, civilians also began to witness these UFOs as they continued to dart across the skies of South Florida. Residents of both Dade and Broward counties began to report strange lights over the Atlantic Ocean and along the Atlantic coast. Commercial radio stations relayed strange reports from local eyewitnesses. Something was definitely happening over the skies of the Sunshine State.

And the reports kept coming. It quickly became apparent to all who lived there that the night of March 31, 1967, was simply the beginning of a major UFO flap that would turn South Florida into a hot spot for unidentified flying objects and leave residents befuddled for years to come.

***

Sarah Hall was excited about her camping trip near the Everglades. It was an opportunity for her boyfriend, Scott, to spend some quality time with her father. Always an outdoors person, Sarah relished the time she spent outside, especially under the stars, but this camping trip would be different than any other, and it would leave her questioning what exactly might be out there among the stars she so loved to gaze at.

It was still cool in March, a perfect time to camp in the area. The Florida sun would not be a problem, and the annoying mosquitoes had not yet materialized in force. The first few days were relaxing and uneventful. On the third evening, she was playing cards with Scott, her father and a few new friends they met on the campgrounds. After a few hours, she and Scott took a break from cards and walked around the campgrounds. The camp park, near Homestead Air Force Base, was a secluded area that gave campers a genuine Florida outdoor experience.

While working their way across a walking trail, Sarah looked up to the sky and saw something with red lights along the side and white light in front rise from the trees approximately half a mile away. Startled, she pointed out the object to Scott as it rose slowly above the tree line and moved horizontally out over the coast for about 10 minutes, all at a very slow pace. When it came over land again, it began to move extremely fast, then slowed down again as it moved towards the coast. Sarah and Scott watched as the object kept up this circular-type pattern for more than an hour. As they sat and watched in amazement, Sarah noted the object made a faint jet engine whine, but she had never seen or heard anything quite like that before.

"Does this thing look like an airplane or helicopter to you?" she asked Scott.

"I have to admit, I've never seen anything like that before," he responded. "The lights are different than an airplane, and it's going way too fast to be a helicopter."

They ran back to the campsite to get Sarah's father, who up until that point was focused on his card hands and did not see the strange object in the sky. The object crossed over a gravel road about a mile east from the campground, closer to the coast, so Sarah made her father drive them down to take a look. On the way, they ran into a Homestead Air Force Base vehicle and a uniformed man who refused to acknowledge the object they were excitedly pointing at.

"You don't see that strange object up there?" she questioned the man.

"There are just some boys out here drinking beer," he radioed to someone at the base. "I've got it under control."

Sarah, never one to suffer foolishness or indignation, said, "Are you seriously not going to look at that thing? Why won't you even look?"

The man in uniform would not let Sarah and her group go any farther down the road, and this really angered her, but Scott quickly cautioned her that this was probably a military matter at this point and that they should not interfere.

Sarah found it profoundly odd that the soldier would not even look over his shoulder, where the craft was clearly visible. Frustrated and still filled with adrenaline, they drove back to camp, at which point Scott took a walkie-talkie with him and walked back down the road to see if he could get closer on foot. The object crossed over the road above him while he was talking with Sarah on the walkie-talkie. Suddenly, the radio cut out and he came running back to the campsite in a state of panic.

"It was right above me and suddenly the radio went dead," he explained in an excited voice. "I just got too spooked out. This whole thing is too creepy."

The radio began to work as soon as the craft moved towards the coast. Eventually, the object dropped down and out of sight, like a balloon landing.

"At the speeds it accelerated to, it was definitely not a balloon, yet it was able to get slow enough to land like one, which made us believe that what we saw wasn't a conventional aircraft," admitted Sarah.

The next morning, when Sarah asked the campground manager whether he saw the strange object, he shrugged it off. "We see a lot of weird things around here," he said. "Nobody pays any attention anymore."

Sarah reported the incident to the National UFO Reporting Center (NUFORC), which is important from an evidential standpoint. Having these accounts on record, especially when they can be corroborated by other similar accounts, goes a long way in proving that, at the very least, something strange did indeed happen and that it was not a figment of some lone person's imagination.

***

Bob King was a paperboy in Miami in 1967, and on the night in question he was finishing his paper route heading north on NW 11th Avenue when he went over a set of train tracks and noticed the sky lit up above him. He first thought someone must have turned on the nearby stadium lights, but as he approached NW 23rd Street to go left to his house, he saw what he first believed to be a gigantic owl perched on top of a building. Startled, he soon realized it was a very bright object moving slowly along the tree line, as if searching for something.

Bob remembers the object being as bright as a crystal chandelier, with glowing rectangular tubes with dark areas in between them and a narrow dark ring around the bottom. He recalls the object being wider in the center than on its sides, and the top of the object remained dark.

"It seemed to drop out of the sky and light up the entire area," he said. "I also heard 'tinging' sounds in sets of three, and I became extremely scared at this point and left my bike on the ground and ran into the back door of my house instead of the front door."

Bob also recalls running from window to window looking out to see if he could sneak a peak at the strange object, which was still lighting up the entire street. Suddenly, the street went dark and the strange sounds stopped.

"I remember crawling into my bed and pulling the covers over my eyes," he said. "I was terrified, and I still get scared when I think about what happened that night."

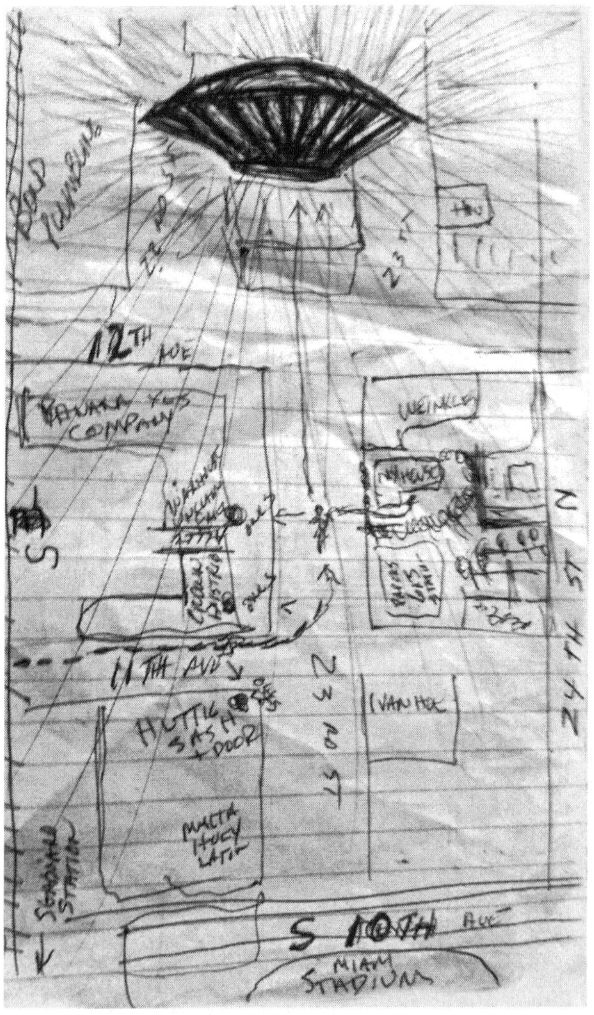

Drawing by Bob King

***

Ramey Air Force Base was a strategic military base located in Aguadilla, Puerto Rico, approximately 60 miles west of San Juan. Established in 1936 in response to U.S. Army Air Corps officials advocating that an air base in Puerto Rico was a necessary and logical defense of the Panama Canal, the base was eventually closed in 1973, but over the years, it served the United States well during several wars and part of the Cold War. It was also home to B-17 Flying Fortresses and B-36 Peacemakers, the biggest warplanes ever to wear an American star. Around the time of the South Florida incident, two airmen at Ramey AFB had an incredible encounter with a UFO and managed to photograph it. It was all part of what was to become one of the biggest UFO flaps ever involving several sightings at U.S. military bases. The official Department of the Air Force report, which was sent to the Foreign Technology Division at Air Force Systems Demand at Wright-Patterson Air Force Base in Ohio, provides myriad details regarding the sighting.

Airmen Padilla and Henry reported a disc-shaped object with two distinct levels (upper and lower deck), about the length of a KC-135 Stratotanker (136 feet in length), with brilliant white lights and a reddish-looking band slightly above the midsection. The object appeared to be floating or hovering just above the water and traveled a short distance from left to right and back. It then began to rise from the water traveling from left to right. It then reversed its flight path and disappeared from view to the northeast. The sighting occurred at the northeast corner of Ramey AFB by the beach and lasted approximately five minutes.

In his comments, Robert D. Williamson, Captain, USAF, Chief, Combat Intelligence ranch, 72nd Bomb Wing (SAC), was of the opinion that "airmen Padilla and Henry are reliable and stable individuals. They are not the publicity-seeking type. Airman Padilla was particularly concerned that other people would think him a 'nut' if his sighting became public. After having discussed this sighting with other members of the Intelligence Division and letting the Prediction and Interpretation Section examine the 35mm slide, this seems to be a creditable sighting incident."

A black and white 8x10 inch photo (above), copied from a 35mm color slide, is included in the Department of the Air Force report. It clearly shows an extremely bright white object in the sky.

***

Beck Willis was driving home from a movie in Hallandale with his younger brother and best friend in the spring of 1967 when he observed a bright light in the distance making some very impressive, highly unorthodox movements across the distant sky.

"Do you guys see that?" he asked his fellow passengers.

As they continued to observe the object, they realized it was getting closer. It quickly raced across the sky only to come to a virtual standstill, then quickly dash across the sky in an entirely different direction, where it would once again appear to stop and hover. They noticed the object had one single bright light and no flashing lights typical of conventional aircraft.

"What in the world is that thing?" Beck wondered. What Beck called this "observational phase" went on for a few minutes before they realized the object was getting too close for comfort, so they pulled off the highway exit ramp and over to the side of the road. They were in an old ragtop VW, so they did not have to get out of the car to witness what they saw next. Much to their astonishment, they saw a single, triangle-shaped object hovering directly over their heads, approximately 500 to 1,000 feet from ground level. It had lights on each of its three points, but none of them blinked, and they were all white/yellow in color. Needless to say, the three boys were blown away. They had never seen or heard of anything like this. As they watched, the object floated silently overhead in a very small circular course, still directly over their heads.

Beck started describing the object verbally so they could remember and validate it afterwards. They could not believe what they were seeing, even though they were all seeing it very clearly with their own eyes. Black and silent, the object would slowly hover over their heads, stop and hover again. It did this for what seemed like an eternity, and because it was a clear night and the boys could see everything, they noticed it did not have any wings, was not a helicopter or any other conventional aircraft for that matter. It was simply a black triangle with no markings or flashing lights of any kind. It was completely silent in the quiet night sky. No prop sounds, no jet sounds.

After watching the object's slow, hypnotic motion for a few more minutes, the boys noticed it stopped circling overhead and began flying away slowly. Then, in the blink of an eye, it shot off into the night sky without so much as emitting a single sound. The boys sat there, astonished, not sure of what to do or say.

"We should get home and tell our parents," said an excited Beck.

"Tell them what exactly?" retorted his friend. He had a point, but Beck was determined to tell his tale to anyone who would listen.

They drove to Beck's house and told the story to his disbelieving mother and father. Beck called the local police department and the Miami International Airport to report what they saw and ask if they had seen this object or traced it on radar. Neither the police nor airport officials had any idea what Beck was talking about. Regardless, the three boys knew what they saw, and they also knew it was not anything that existed from a conventional standpoint.

Over the years, the three witnesses learned to remain silent about the incident, as the usual response was one of disbelief and doubt. This did not bother Beck so much because if he did not see it with his own eyes, he would not have believed it either. He knows what they saw that night was not only real but also extraordinary.

As he described in his report to the National UFO Reporting Center (NUFORC) in 1999, "Needless to say, I am convinced what we saw over 30 years ago was definitely not of this Earth."

***

Pilot Robert Halpern was at the Doral Beach Hotel in Miami in mid-July 1967 when he and his wife witnessed several UFOs. He describes the incident as follows:

> *We were on the roof of the Doral Beach Hotel cabana building, above the swimming pool deck and overlooking the beach and ocean. I was looking straight north toward the Fort Lauderdale area when I saw three lights in the sky and asked my wife what she thought was moving down the coastline towards us at a very high rate of speed. We both observed these lights pass directly over us so quickly that we had to instantly turn 180 degrees to the south to follow the path of the lights over our location and proceed on over South Miami Beach, where the lights took an instant turn to the left and followed on a straight line east over the Atlantic Ocean, where they simply disappeared.*

Robert noted he had done a lot of flying prior to this sighting and was in continuous contact with both military and civilian aircraft manufacturers during his career. It was simply not possible, he said, for him to know if the lights he saw were all on one craft or three different craft. The synchronicity of the movement, seemingly low altitude, absolute lack of sound, and instant change of direction caused him to believe this sighting was of nothing he could identify as operating within the aerodynamic physics of anything made on Earth. He and his now ex-wife believed this to possibly be a single, or three, unidentified flying objects, and not likely an optical illusion of some kind.

Some years later, Robert learned about the South Florida UFO flap at a MUFON presentation given by Bill Schroeder. Robert asked him if he thought his sighting could have been connected to what he and Dennis experienced the night of March 31, 1967. Although they may never know for sure, it was proposed that it could have been a follow-up rec-con flight. One thing is for certain, the amount of UFO activity in South Florida during the winter and spring of 1967 strongly suggests "something" was happening, but witnesses can only speculate what that "something" may have been.

On April 22, 2014, Robert experienced another UFO sighting in Lakeland, Fla., with three other witnesses, which further validated what he and his ex-wife saw 47 years earlier. His current wife described the incident to MUFON, which can be found in the network's report database as Case Number 55702. The report states:

> *Tuesday evening at 8:15 p.m. ... My neighbor and his father were out in front of their house. I went outside to talk to him. He and his father had just seen three objects flying over. He said, "Look, a UFO!" We looked to the northwest and saw two red-orange lights in the sky coming over the tree line. Behind the two lights was a large black triangle with no light. As they went overhead with no sound whatsoever, you could see that the red-*

orange light was in the center of the two other large black triangles. As we watched, the middle object with the red-orange light slowly went out. We watched the three objects slowly fly to the southeast in a row until they were out of site. My neighbor ran home to get his phone so he could take a video just in case another one flew over. At that time I yelled to (Robert) to come outside. A couple of minutes later, all three of us saw two more black triangles with red-orange lights flying in the same direction, again with no sound whatsoever. My friend took a video of the last one coming over the tree line. About that same time we saw an airplane to the south of us flying in an easterly direction. You can hear the airplane in the background of his video. We saw no more after that.

In some ways, Robert's 2014 sighting is even more spectacular due to the proximity and clearer view of the unidentified objects. Having significant UFO encounters almost 50 years apart is something not lost on Robert. "The 2014 sighting is as much proof of extraterrestrial activity as I need," he said. "The difference is that after the 1967 sighting, we were afraid to talk to anyone about it out of fear of being ridiculed. Since this most recent incident occurred, we've been talking to anyone who will listen and have been probing for answers using every avenue available to us. People are more open to it nowadays."

***

The day after Schroeder and Force's UFO encounter, some 200 miles to the northwest in Tampa, 16-year-old Doug Farber saw something strange in the skies over his house. He was standing in his front yard at about 9 p.m. when he noticed a large, blue-green light in the northwestern sky.

"What made me look closer was that the light was moving at a very fast rate of speed," he recalled. "It took perhaps 20 to 30 seconds to move from the northwestern horizon to the northeastern horizon, at which time I lost sight of it."

With MacDill Air Force Base about 25 miles to the southwest of his position, Doug saw jet aircraft on a daily basis. F-4s flew regularly in the area at that time, so he knew about how long it took for aircraft to move across the sky. The light Doug saw was large enough that, if it was from an aircraft, he would have heard the engines.

"I went inside and told my dad what I had seen, and he told me to call the sheriff's department," said Doug. "I did, and they told me to call MacDill Air Force Base."

When Doug called and explained what he saw, the man asked where he lived, thanked him and hung up. About 15 to 20 minutes later, three Air Force jets flew directly over his house, traveling from the southwest to the northeast where the light disappeared.

"I don't know what it was that I saw, but I felt then and still feel now that the object was unusual and not conventional," Doug asserted. "I wasn't on drugs or anything like that, because I know some people would not give any credence to what a 16-year-old kid said about seeing a UFO in 1967."

Doug has often wondered what it was he saw. Seeing the strange light in and of itself was not a big deal, but the way the Air Force responded to his call, and apparently scrambled three jets to intercept the object, was a big deal, and it suggested to him he did indeed see a genuine unidentified craft that was of particular interest to the Air Force. Years later, Doug finally reported the incident to the National UFO Reporting Center.

***

The UFO activity in and around South Florida in 1967 was indeed brisk. Both civilians and military personnel reported sightings ranging from bright lights to disc-shaped, triangle-shaped and cigar-shaped craft, and all moving at speeds and in ways that defied the laws of conventional aerodynamics and physics of the time.

Most eyewitness reports about UFO sightings during the winter and spring of 1967 were done so in a vacuum, meaning one person really did not know other similar incidents were occurring across the region. It was not until years later that information regarding the Cuban MiG-21s came out, and, because their hands were basically tied as military and public service employees, it took Schroeder and Force years to piece together some of the strange sightings that took place in the days and months following their encounter.

Chapter Six

School Daze

Crestview Elementary School sits four miles northeast of the Miami-Opa locka Airport, which in 1967 was the world's busiest civilian airport and also the location of a U.S. Coast Guard Air/Sea Rescue Station, one of the nation's first Naval Aviation Reserve Bases, the headquarters for several CIA covert operations, and a Federal Aviation Administration (FAA) installation. Also, about three miles to the west-southwest of the school was the Nike Hercules Missile Site, where anti-aircraft missiles stood at the ready to protect the southeastern United States from a potential Soviet nuclear bomber attack launched from Cuba.

As a result of the school's precarious location, a huge concentration of radio transmitter towers surrounded it. According to dozens of accounts, several UFOs were spotted both close to and directly above the school on April 6, 7, and 8, 1967, less than a week after Schroeder and Force's UFO encounters at their respective military bases.

Irving Lillien, Ph.D., who investigated the incident for the Aerial Phenomena Research Organization (APRO), interviewed several witnesses and provided a detailed report to the organization. In his report, he noted that, "the sightings at Crestview may prove to be among the most important recorded since the objects were seen by over 200 children and adults for prolonged periods of time over a period of several days in broad daylight."

Lillien also mentioned that, although many aerial objects such as airplanes, helicopters and blimps proliferated the skies around that area due to its proximity to Miami-Opa locka Airport, the witnesses were absolutely sure that the phenomena they observed were completely unlike anything they had seen before.

The May-June 1967 APRO Bulletin published an abbreviated version of Lillien's report, and several other publications, including *The Miami Herald*, *The Miami News*, and the *National Enquirer* (whose tagline in those days was "The World's Liveliest Paper"), published various accounts in the following days and months.

According to Lillien's report, the first sighting took place on Thursday, April 6, and was made by 33-year-old Robert Apfel, a teacher at Crestview, and several of his students. At 12:45 p.m., the witnesses were outside a portable classroom when they spotted an aluminum-appearing, slightly reflective ellipsoid that Apfel described as "two lenses back to back with no markings, lights or details." He also noted that it appeared stationary, about 60 feet above the ground over a telephone pole and about a mile away, and the size of a 50-cent piece at arm's length. As Apfel and the children watched, the object suddenly disappeared. No sound, air movement or shadows were observed.

At about 8:30 a.m. the following morning, Apfel arrived at his classroom when "the children – some excited, some crying and some hysterical – said they had seen something." Apfel calmed his class down and had them sketch what they saw. The drawings, he said, generally agreed with one another and depicted a turreted structure among the tops of the trees. (These drawings, incidentally, were later turned over to investigators from Homestead Air Force Base.) The object was approximately 150 to 200 yards away in a field directly north of the school. It too disappeared suddenly. Later that day, when Apfel learned of yet another sighting near the school, he closed the window blinds in his classroom to avoid further commotion and upset amongst his students.

At 9:45 a.m. that same day, 12-year-old Andy Cohen was in his classroom when some girls rushed in and said flying saucers were being watched. Cohen ran outside and noticed several teachers and students milling around, looking to the north beyond the school fence. Teachers were trying to get the children lined up in an orderly manner when Cohen spotted four cigar-shaped objects with white lights on each end. One hovered over the trees, went down behind them, and then took off again. Another came straight across the sky going up and down in a wavy motion. And yet another seemed to be chasing an airplane. They eventually all went off at an angle and disappeared.

Most of the children described the objects as white, although Cohen claimed there was one white, one black, one red, and one silver. The craft had no markings, portholes, domes or other lights, and they never changed shape or made any kind of sound. Several children called local newspapers after school that day, and it was Cohen's call that actually alerted *The Miami Herald*, which resulted in a brief media frenzy.

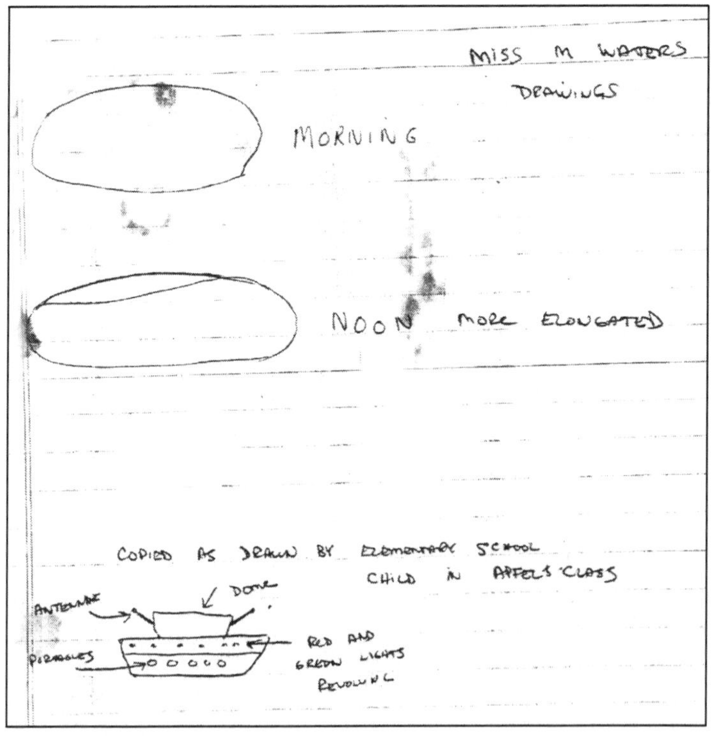

Numerous Crestview Elementary witnesses provided testimony to NICAP, including the above drawings from teacher Marion Waters and a student of Robert Apfel's class.

As Mike Petit, *Miami Herald* staff writer wrote in the newspaper's April 8 edition, "Little girls screamed, boys pointed and teachers followed anxious fingers to the object above the treetops … It was *Twilight Zone*, *The Invaders*, and *Outer Limits* all rolled into one, five-minute show. Only this time, said 12-year-old Andy Cohen, 'it was for real.'"

Sixth-grade teacher Virginia Martin was not paying attention at first because she was attempting to get her students lined up, but most of the girls and boys at morning recess already were running towards the schoolyard fence, yelling to Mrs. Martin, "You've got to look! You've got to look!"

Mrs. Martin did, and she could not believe what she saw. She described the craft as oval-shaped and hovering. She told the *Herald* that, "I realized that an airplane doesn't do that. I thought, my gosh, this couldn't be happening."

Some of the other children who Lillien interviewed got the impression that the UFOs were hiding because they would move up above and then down behind the trees. One of the boys, John McCleary, 11, noticed the objects "milling around amongst the trees, circling and whipping around in fast, jerky motions." He also observed that they would come back, land, go behind the trees, and then do it all over again.

Lillien, who recalls seeing a few uniformed Air Force personnel out on the streets by the school, says the children he spoke to were very energized and excited, as were their parents. "There were literally hundreds of children and adults who viewed these vehicles' antics over the course of several days," he remembers. "I have not the slightest reason to doubt the truthfulness of all involved. The circumstances pretty well rule out the possibility of deception here. The children gave the impression of seeing something quite important; they were very persuasive."

***

On the next day, Saturday, April 8, several people experienced a similar sighting at the same general location as Crestview Elementary School. Local resident John Wolf, 42, shared his account with *The Miami News*, which published it in their April 13 edition. According to Wolf, he was driving up to his house when he saw his daughter in the driveway. Having already heard from other neighbors, she told him excitedly, "They're back."

Wolf quickly found his binoculars in the house, piled his four kids into his truck, and drove over to a field near Crestview Elementary, where he found 30 to 40 people standing around on a dead end road adjacent to the field. They were looking north, and when Wolf looked up he saw three or four objects hovering just behind a row of trees. According to Wolf, they seemed to be changing shape from oval to cigar-shape and back again. The objects, which also seemed to change size, had what looked like the "glass dome of a coffee pot" on their tops.

Wolf also remembers seeing airplanes from North Perry Airport flying around at the same time, and while he could easily see the details on these conventional craft, he saw no such details on the UFOs. And every time a plane approached them, they simply disappeared as if turning off a light. None of the witnesses detected any motion associated with these disappearing acts; the objects simply vanished and then reappeared in the same spot once the airplanes flew a comfortable distance away.

Wolf watched the objects for about an hour, describing them as "pogo sticks jumping all over the sky." He decided to go home and tell his wife what was happening, but she simply laughed, thinking he was playing a joke on her. He convinced her to go back with him, and when they arrived at the field again, she was not laughing anymore. There they were, in full sight, on a bright clear day, zipping and zinging around as if playing a game of tag. Wolf, who lived in the area for many years, was used to seeing airplanes and helicopters because of the local airports, so he knew these things did not resemble anything close to the conventional craft he was used to seeing.

Another interesting thing Wolf noted was there was absolutely no sound and no exhaust emanating from any of the strange objects. He was fascinated by, not scared of, these unknown craft, and he really wanted to know what in the world he was looking at. After several more minutes, the unknowns ceased their activity and slowly moved away and out of sight.

For an hour and a half, Wolf and 40 other people watched these objects, on a very clear day, maneuvering around the sky. They all described the craft in similar fashion, and they were all certain of what they saw. The whole thing befuddled Wolf, who previously spent eight years in the Navy and was a plane captain on a flight service line.

"I'm too old to be flippy about these things," he told reporters. "I'd like to know what they were, even if someone proves I was having hallucinations."

A few days later, the Air Force officially reported that what everybody saw in the sky was simply a Coast Guard helicopter on a training mission. The *National Enquirer* noted in its June 25 edition that when the Air Force report was published in *The Miami Herald* on April 11, residents of the Crestview area were "shocked and infuriated," and many of them felt the report "reflected unfavorably on their veracity and that of their children."

Andy Cohen told *The Miami Herald* that if his "cigars" were helicopters, you would have been able to see something that looked like overhead rotors. Plus, only one of the four objects Cohen saw was white – the color of the Coast Guard helicopter the Air Force said was the culprit.

Robert Apfel was firm in his belief that what he saw was a "flying saucer" and remained in complete disagreement with the Air Force, as did the principal of Crestview Elementary School, Priscilla Pierson, who observed, "I don't believe in calling white or black something else. I didn't see the objects, but I certainly believe my children and teachers."

John Gramlich was a University of Miami senior and a member of the National Investigation Committee on Aerial Phenomena (NICAP), a group that investigated UFO sightings around the country, during the time of the mass sighting. Gramlich interviewed Crestview area residents at length immediately following the sightings and told both the *Enquirer* and the *Homestead News Leader*: "I am convinced it wasn't a helicopter. I can't see how anyone could think it was a helicopter."

But the Air Force stuck to its guns, sending out a news release on April 10 to state as much. The release, which originated from "United States Air Force, Headquarters 19th Bombardment Wing (SAC), Directorate of Information, Homestead Air Force Base," stated:

> *The Air Force has completed an investigation of the UFO sighting by the students and teachers of Crestview Elementary School of 2201 NW 187th St., at 9:45, April 7th. The majority of the witnesses described the object as white with a red light that flashed once. The object was sighted along a line north-northwest of the school. Witnesses differed as to the size and distance of the object. The investigation revealed that a Coast Guard helicopter, white with red trim, was maneuvering in the area of North Perry Airport between 9:31 a.m. and 11:07 a.m. the morning of the report. The helicopter was practicing landings and takeoffs in an East-West direction between ground level and 1000 feet altitude. North Perry Airport is almost due North of the elementary school and approximately three miles in distance.*
>
> *The Air Force concludes that given the time of the day with the angle of the Sun and the unfamiliar maneuvering of the white and red helicopter, the witnesses could not identify it as such. As to the number of objects sighted, the*

white and red objects was the only consistent description given. The Air Force attributes the other objects to the high number of small aircraft activity in the vicinity of North Perry Airport.

John Wolf and the other witnesses were having none of it. "There were no Coast Guard helicopters up in the sky that day, not one," said Wolf. "They certainly won't sell me a bill of goods that I was watching airplanes or helicopters."

***

Elizabeth Holloway was a sixth-grader at Crestview Elementary School when the incident took place. She recalls that during recess in April 1967, she and hundreds of other students from Crestview, as well as a few teachers, witnessed three oval-shaped objects coming through a few clouds on a mostly clear day, directly overhead.

"We watched as the two smaller of the objects appeared to be dancing around the larger oval-shaped object coming down towards us," she remembered. "The larger object seemed to be the size of a cruise ship, but its shape was more oval or cigar-shaped and it was shiny metal like. I saw the large object land in the field near the school. I didn't see where the other two objects went."

After what seemed like hours, Holloway and her classmates were told to go home. She was actually one of the dozens of students who rode their bikes to the landing area not far from the school. "We stepped over a berm and found a field of weeds and grass that appeared to be charred and smashed into an oval shape," she said. "The area seemed to be the size of a large boat. There was no object there, but it looked like the remains of something that had recently been laying there."

Before long, men in uniforms and the press started interviewing Holloway and her friends. She listened to a boy who shared the same account she did. The following day, she remembers reading *The Miami Herald* story and the Air Force conclusion that it was a helicopter on maneuvers.

"I knew otherwise," she said, "but I understand now that the Air Force had to say what they did in order to avoid mass hysteria. In those days, people were not comfortable with the idea of unknown objects flying in and around their communities. You have to remember that we had just been through the Cuban Missile Crisis, and we also heard a lot of reports about UFOs in those days, so we weren't sure if these things were friendly or not."

Years later, Holloway took her children to the location of the sighting, as they had heard their mother talk about it many times. "It was the 1990s, and we discovered that a football stadium was built directly on the spot where I saw that UFO land in 1967," she said. "Come to think of it, the UFO was about the size of the stadium floor!"

In 2011, Holloway made an official report of her sighting to the National UFO Reporting Center (NUFORC).

***

Frank Grayson did not witness any UFOs around Crestview Elementary School in April 1967, but he does remember the incident as one of the strangest things ever to occur in the Miami area. "This was a highly populated area," he said, "and people need to realize that an elementary school was closed because of UFOs! The entire school witnessed the event, including teachers, administrators and students – hundreds of people."

Grayson, who verified the incident with NUFORC, was concerned because he had an uncle who lived on Opa locka Boulevard at the time, and he could not get home for lunch from work via his normal route because the roads were blocked and detours were set up. He said his uncle definitely saw something that day but would never talk to him about it. And anyone he may have talked to has long since passed.

"I remember hearing that the UFO actually landed, and I've always asked myself how this could have happened in a populated, modern country and yet the incident is all but forgotten now," he said. "My god, how many more of these events have taken place and time has simply swept them under the rug?"

***

Dmitry Alexander, an assistant professor in the audiovisual department at Miami-Dade Junior College, and his wife, Kathleen, lived approximately six blocks northeast of Crestview Elementary School. At 8:15 p.m. on April 27, 1967, Dmitry saw some strange lights while driving home from work. When he arrived home, he found his binoculars and watched as these objects flew in a clockwise circle several miles wide. He saw as few as six and as many as 10 at a given time and could not hear any sounds emanating from them.

He noticed the lights were strange. White, green and red, the lights were all in a line, and they didn't change when the craft changed direction. Dmitry recalls it was as if the lights were on a string. Kathleen, now watching the strange lights with him, noticed the shape of these objects was different than an airplane. Now convinced they were not conventional aircraft, Dmitry called the Highway Patrol.

"Some bored sergeant answered," Dmitry later told the *National Enquirer*. "He gave me the phone number of a lieutenant at Homestead Air Force Base. When I reached him, he said he'd have someone call me back in five minutes. After about 40 minutes, I phoned *The Miami Herald*. Nobody was interested."

While Dmitry was making his futile phone calls, Kathleen watched two of the objects move straight down. When Dmitry came outside again, another one dropped from sight in the same rapid manner. He was now deeply troubled and wanted to know what was going on. He called the lieutenant again, who was surprised that nobody had called him back. He told Dmitry someone would call him back promptly, and 20 minutes later a sergeant called and started asking questions. The following day, a military helicopter flew low over the area, but nobody talked to Dmitry or his wife.

On May 8, 10 days after Dmitry first contacted the Air Force base, an officer from the base called and asked to speak to him. Kathleen told him her husband was at the college. When the officer called Dmitry, he told him that his report was marked "urgent" but someone had lost it. The incident, nevertheless, needed to be investigated, and he asked Dmitry when they could meet.

The next morning, Dmitry met the officer and once again answered several of the same type of questions the sergeant asked. They discussed the strange sighting, and the officer actually told him that some sightings defied explanation. Because Miami was so close to Cuba, Dmitry was concerned about the possibility of unfriendly foreign intruders, a common sentiment in 1967. He also noted that Crestview was close to the ocean and asked if planes could come in beneath radar. The officer told him it was impossible.

Dmitry and his wife, like many of the other North Miami UFO witnesses, were left with more questions than answers. However frustrated, they eventually went on with their normal lives, their minds far away from thoughts of UFOs, extraterrestrials and other extraordinary things.

***

During an approximately three-month period in 1967, a flurry of activity descended upon Crestview Elementary School and the South Florida region. Based on dozens of reliable witness testimonies, several unknown objects performed strange maneuvers in the sky, changed shape, and even disappeared only to reappear moments later. Whether or not one or more of these mysterious craft actually landed in a field near Crestview Elementary School remains a mystery. Some witnesses said they thought one of the objects had landed, while others simply saw the objects hovering over a row of trees.

As far as the Air Force's official explanation of what witnesses saw near Crestview, many questions remain. If indeed a white Coast Guard helicopter with red trim was maneuvering in the area of North Perry Airport between 9:31 a.m. and 11:07 a.m. on the morning of April 7, and this is the official explanation of what hundreds of eyewitnesses saw, why did Robert Apfel and his students see several objects at 8:30 a.m., and what did they see the day before? It also does not explain what John Wolf and 40 others saw on April 8 and what Dmitry and Kathleen Alexander saw in March.

William Allen, a reporter for the *Enquirer*, actually spoke to Captain Reed, the Coast Guard pilot who supposedly flew the helicopter in question on the morning of April 7, and he seemed bewildered by his apparent role in the events. He did state that all of his practice maneuvers were performed at North Perry Airport, which is about three miles north of the school. At that distance, however, the helicopter would have looked like a dot, not the large objects described by the children and teachers. Captain Reed, strangely enough, also stated that he was never interviewed by any Air Force investigators, or any military personnel for that matter, regarding the incident.

Combined with the March 31 series of incidents involving B Battery in Key West, Homestead Air Force Base and the Cuban Air Force, it strains credulity to think it was business as usual in South Florida in the spring of 1967. Instead, it is much more plausible, from an objective standpoint, to believe something quite significant was taking place. Something that would cause great consternation for the U.S. military, as well as the Cuban military, and that would affect the lives of hundreds of military personnel and civilians who would question what they saw for the rest of their lives.

But the real questions remain: What were these things? Were they U.S. or Soviet military aircraft? This simply is not plausible because even our most sophisticated aircraft today (never mind 50 years ago) could never come close to the speeds and maneuverability displayed by these objects. Were they extraterrestrial? And if so, why were they so focused in this area? The weather is beautiful in Florida in the spring, but a much more serious explanation is required to validate the presence of extraterrestrial craft that were either searching for something or extremely interested in the military defense apparatus operating in the region at that time.

Could they have lost one of their own craft, as Schroeder suggests, and were simply engaging in a huge search and rescue operation? Or maybe, based on our nuclear capabilities and the fact we came extremely close to waging an all-out nuclear war with the Soviet Union and its allies during the Cuban Missile Crisis just a few years earlier, these advanced beings were simply making sure we did not annihilate all life on the planet.

Schroeder and the other witnesses will probably never know what these things were or what they were doing in the skies over South Florida, but they were left with an interesting mystery to mull over for years to come. For the civilians who shared their experiences with others, it must have been frustrating to know that some people did not give their accounts an ounce of credence. For Schroeder and the other military personnel who were told to remain silent, they would be left to internalize the experience for years and question what they were taught to believe as "real" and within the realm of our current reality.

Eventually, Schroeder would do his own research and talk to other witnesses of the South Florida events or who had similar experiences that occurred at other locations across the country. He would also learn he and his cousin were not the only military witnesses to high strangeness involving UFOs.

Chapter Seven

The UFO Flap of 1967

As it turns out, Schroeder's 1967 UFO encounter was one of many that occurred that year. According to Francis Ridge, NICAP (National Investigations Committee on Aerial Phenomena) Site Coordinator, 1967 encompassed a major part of the most intensive and long-lasting UFO sighting waves of all time.

"It was a U.S. and international UFO sighting wave that actually began in 1966," explained Ridge. "Not only was this a massive sighting wave involving nuclear-equipped missile shutdowns, but there were also a number of humanoid incidents reported, along with the usual ground and air sightings."

Richard H. Hall was a leading Ufologist and proponent of the extraterrestrial hypothesis to explain UFO sightings. In an abstract he wrote titled *1967: The Overlooked UFO Wave and the Colorado*

Project, he stated that the "Great UFO Wave of 1967" is not exactly on the tip of everyone's tongue. In fact, he said, few people even know it happened and even fewer have studied it in any systematic way.

According to Air Force statistics, 1967 ranks as the fourth highest in terms of total UFO reports (exceeded only by 1952, 1966 and 1957, in that order). Even though there was an all-time peak of interest in UFOs around 1967 (with major institutions like the U.S. Congress, the news media and the scientific community engaged in open debate about UFO sightings), the official view of the United States Air Force was all UFOs could be explained as mistaken observations of stars, aircraft and balloons.

Regardless of this rather deficient explanation, NICAP received 3,340 UFO reports in 1967, 273 of which could be labeled as "substantial" cases. In that same period, the Air Force received 937 raw reports, 19 of which were categorized as "unidentified." Independent research conducted by Ted Bloecher and David Webb pinpointed at least 108 humanoid occupant cases worldwide, wherein more-or-less human-like beings were seen in association with UFOs.

UFO sightings were also numerous in other countries in 1967. Although it is difficult to obtain exact figures, the following statement appeared in the book, *UFOs from Behind the Iron Curtain*: " ... 1967 appears likewise (as was 1966) to have been a busy one for UFOs in the Soviet Union, and at the beginning of 1968, *Soviet Weekly* published an article that in the previous year in South Russia alone there had been more than 200 reliable reports of UFO observations." In 1968, *Flying Saucer Report,* a British amateur astronomer publication, summarized 70 UFO cases from England during the summer and fall of 1967. The British Defense Ministry reported 362 cases for 1967 with 46 labeled as "unexplained."

Some interesting, and sobering, facts are linked to 1967, which may explain why UFOs were spotted so frequently and over so many missile bases. That year, the Strategic Air Command reached a level of 1,000 operational Minuteman and 55 Titan II intercontinental ballistic missiles (ICBMs), and the Navy reached a level of 656 submarine-launched ballistic missiles (SLBMs). As part of Projects Latchkey and Crosstie, the United States conducted 85 nuclear tests in 1967-68 and also stockpiled 30,893 nuclear warheads. The Soviet Union, determined to keep up with the United States in the nuclear arms race and grow its own stockpile of warheads, conducted 17 nuclear tests in the Kazakhstan region and stockpiled approximately 45,000 nuclear warheads. The Cold War reached a fever pitch that threatened the destruction of the entire planet. The U.S. national security policy at the time, Mutually Assured Destruction (MAD), most accurately described the prevailing attitude in military circles. Add to this the fact the Arabs and Israelis were engaged in yet more bloodshed, the Six-Day War, and it was clear to anyone who was watching that we learned absolutely nothing from previous wars and conflicts.

Seen through the eyes of an extraterrestrial race that may have had a vested interest in our survival (or in ensuring that we never delivered nuclear weapons to space), it was a precarious time on this planet. Unfortunately, human beings have always behaved like childish barbarians, but now we had the weapons to do serious damage. If extraterrestrial beings were visiting us at the time, they would probably have taken a keen interest in our stockpile of weapons of mass destruction, if only so they could reconnoiter and protect themselves when our fighter jets scrambled to intercept them or our anti-aircraft missiles took aim at them.

Carl Sagan, iconic astronomer, astrophysicist, cosmologist and author, broached this topic brilliantly on his groundbreaking television series, "Cosmos: A Personal Voyage." The series, which aired on PBS in 1980, covered a wide range of scientific topics, including space exploration accomplishments, the origin of life, and a perspective of our place in the universe. In the final episode, "Who Speaks For Earth," Sagan shared the following thoughts regarding the Cold War and the fragile state of humanity:

> *How would we explain all this to a dispassionate extraterrestrial observer? What account would be given of our stewardship of the planet Earth? We have heard the rationales offered by the superpowers. We know who speaks for the nations, but who speaks for the human species? Who speaks for earth? …*
>
> *… From an extraterrestrial perspective, our global civilization is clearly on the edge of failure in the most important task it faces – preserving the lives and well-being of its citizens and the future habitability of the planet. But if we are to live with the growing likelihood of nuclear war, shouldn't we also be willing to explore, vigorously, every possible means to prevent nuclear war? Shouldn't we consider, in every nation, major changes in the traditional*

ways of doing things, a fundamental restructuring of economic, political, social, and religious institutions?

Whether Sagan was simply using the possibility of an extraterrestrial perspective to get his point across, or he truly believed (or knew) extraterrestrial races were indeed observing our madness, has remained a source of debate over the years. And, of course, we can only guess as to what the extraterrestrial perspective might have been in 1967, or in 1980, or even today, but as we look at some of the more compelling UFO encounters of 1967, it is hard not to notice the relationship between missile bases (and other military facilities) and the presence of UFOs that, in some instances, did more than simply showcase advanced flight capabilities and jaw-dropping aerodynamic maneuvers.

***

In the spring of 1967, Robert Salas was stationed at Malmstrom Air Force Base in Montana, where he served as a Deputy Missile Combat Crew Commander (DMCCC) at a Minuteman Launch Control Facility (LCF). During the early morning hours of March 24, while on duty at Oscar Flight launch control center, he received a call from his Flight Security Officer (FSC), who was on duty topside. The FSC informed Salas that he and the guards on duty observed some unidentified flying objects in the vicinity. He also told him they had already flown over the LCF a few times.

Salas recalled the conversation, which he also included in his book, *Faded Giant: The 1967 Missile/UFO Incidents.*

FSC: Sir, we've been seeing some strange lights up here.

Salas: What kind of lights?

FSC: They are … uh … flying around over the site. They aren't aircraft.

Salas: What do they look like?

FSC: Well, they're just lights flying around making some strange maneuvers.

Salas: You mean they're UFOs?

FSC: Well, something like that. All we can tell is they're not aircraft.

Salas: Great. You just keep watching them and let me know if they get any closer.

At first, Salas wondered whether the air security personnel topside might be having some fun with him, but a few minutes later, when his FSC called back in an agitated and distraught state, Salas knew this was no joke.

FSC: Sir, there's one hovering outside the front gate!

Salas: One what?

FSC: A UFO! It's just sitting there. We're all just looking at it. What do you want us to do?

Salas: What? What does it look like?

FSC: I can't really describe it. It's glowing red. What are we supposed to do?

Salas: Make sure the site is secure and I'll phone the Command Post.

FSC: Sir, I have to go now. One of the guys just got injured.

Immediately waking his commander, Lt. Fred Meiwald, Salas relayed the phone conversations. Within seconds, the missiles began changing from "Alert" status to "No-Go" status. He recalls that all 10 missiles had shut down in rapid succession. When a missile went off alert status, it was usually due to a power outage at a particular site, so the site power generator would come on line and pick up the power load, fixing the issue.

He knew it was extremely rare, however, for more than one missile to go offline for any length of time. In this instance, none of the missiles came back online, and he realized the problem was not caused by a lack of power, but by some kind of signal that had been sent to the missiles.

After Meiwald reported the incident to the command post, Salas phoned a security guard to determine what had transpired topside. He told Salas that another guard who approached the UFO was injured, albeit not seriously. Salas does not recall the exact nature of the injuries, but he does remember the guard was removed from the base by helicopter. Meiwald later learned that one of the other security guards was so terrified by the incident that he was released from further guard duty.

Meiwald also informed Salas that a week earlier, on March 16, the same exact scenario played out at another launch control center (Echo Flight), approximately 20 miles away. Here, too, a UFO was spotted by security guards hovering over the site. Suddenly, and within a matter of seconds, 10 ICBMs reported a "No-Go" status in rapid succession.

Later that morning, Salas and his exhausted crew were relieved by their scheduled replacement crew. The missiles had not yet been brought back online by on-site maintenance, which was a serious concern. Once topside, Salas tracked down his FSC and spoke with him directly.

Salas: Were you telling me the truth about the UFOs?

FSC: It was no joke sir. I swear, it was right out there.

Salas: What did it look like?

FSC: It was like a big red-orange ball. It was so bright that it was hard to get a good look at it. But it was there for about a couple of minutes after we talked then it just took off.

Salas: What about the man who was injured?

FSC: It wasn't too bad.

The FSC went on to tell Salas the guard had been injured trying to run from the UFO by jumping the fence and cut his hand on the barbed wire. The UFO did not attack the guards in any way.

When Salas returned to the base, he and Meiwald discussed the incident with their squadron commander, Col. George Eldridge, and an Air Force investigator from the Air Force Office of Special Investigations (AFOSI). Neither Col. Eldridge nor the AFOSI investigator were able to explain the incident, nor were they able to confirm that it was some kind of readiness exercise. Salas could tell that Col. Eldridge, an experienced WWII veteran who was well liked by everyone in the squadron, was truly baffled by these strange events. After completing the briefing, Salas and Meiwald were told that the incident was to be considered highly classified and that they were not to discuss it with anyone, including their spouses or fellow crewmembers.

From that moment until the time of Salas's transfer from Malmstrom in June 1969, none of the crews received any information about the incident. He recalls that there was never a report of investigation released to the missile crews, nor was there any other explanation given. Salas knew this was unusual because they were usually given regular briefings about any technical areas of concern regarding the readiness of their weapons.

Sworn to secrecy, Salas did not speak to anyone about the incident for 27 years. In 1994, he thought the incident had become declassified after reading about it in the Timothy Good book, *Above Top Secret.* As a result, Salas started to perform his own research, which would be the fodder for his book, *Faded Giant.* Eventually, he spoke to the DMCCC in command of Echo Flight on the night in question. He told Salas that prior to the shutdown of his missiles, he received more than one report from security patrols and maintenance crews about UFO sightings in the vicinity. They also told him one of the objects hovered directly above one of the launch sites.

Further discussions with individuals from Boeing – who provided technical assistance and performed additional tests during the investigation of these shutdowns – revealed to Salas there was never a resolution as to the cause or explanation of these incidents. The written unit history of the 341st Missile Wing from 1967 also confirmed that conclusion.

In a paper written for public release, Salas summarized his thoughts on the matter: "Since the termination of Project Blue Book, the Air Force has maintained the position that no reported UFO incident has ever affected national security. The incident I described above clearly had national security implications. The Air Force has clearly and deliberately hidden the fact that a large number of Air Force personnel reported sighting UFOs at the time many of our strategic missiles became, unaccountably, disabled."

Looking back on the incident now, Salas remembers how intimidated he felt immediately following the event. "After we were relieved by another crew, we were ordered to return to the base immediately," he explained. "I wanted to take some time to discuss the incident with the flight security officer who I had spoken to on the phone about the incident and wanted to go over the details, but he seemed reluctant to speak with me, probably because he already had been ordered not to discuss it with me at length."

Salas also recalls how Meiwald kept trying to push him out the door to the waiting helicopter. When they arrived back at the base for their debriefing with Col. Eldridge, Salas could tell that the usually cool Eldridge looked nervous and his face lacked color.

"I asked him what was going on, and he simply shook his head and said he did not know," recounted Salas. "We were then ordered to sign non-disclosure statements by another officer who worked for AFOSI. I tried to object, stating we already had high security clearances and were subject to security regulations. However, he insisted."

The AFOSI officer also made a point of showing Salas and Meiwald paragraphs in the statement about penalties, which included prison and heavy fines, if they disclosed any of what had happened the previous night. They were then verbally reminded not to speak to anyone about what happened, including spouses, friends or anyone at all, and there was no time limit to that confidentiality.

The next morning, Salas received a telephone call at home from a security guard who saw the object during the incident. He pleaded with Salas to meet with him and some other guards to discuss what happened. They were looking for some answers to what they saw. "I told him I was under non-disclosure restrictions and could not meet with him," said Salas. "It was very difficult for me to take that position because he was clearly distressed by the event."

At that point, two things became very clear to Salas. First, something highly unusual occurred that could not be explained, and the USAF wanted the incident kept well-hidden from any internal or external discussion. Second, it was his duty and responsibility to maintain secrecy.

"I, too, wanted more answers and, from what I knew about the way the Minuteman missile system worked, what happened should not have happened," explained Salas. "It was an extraordinary event. I didn't like it, but I would do my best to keep the secret because I saw myself as a professional officer who followed orders."

In the following days, weeks and months, Salas and the other witnesses heard nothing more in their pre-tour briefings about that night, any follow-up investigations, or any engineering evaluations. As a result, it made Salas even more curious as to what exactly transpired.

In a recent brief Salas wrote titled, "UFOs and the Nuclear Connection," he talks about how, ever since the atomic bomb was dropped on Hiroshima in July 1945, UFOs have been seen, tracked by radar, and even engaged by fighter jets at missile bases across the United States. He goes on to hold the United States Air Force accountable for being part of a "ruse to discount and discredit the many incidents, including the Malmstrom AFB incidents, which demonstrated the reality of UFOs."

Salas points out that the Condon Report, the infamous "scientific investigation" conducted by the University of Colorado (under contract for the Air Force), was never meant to look for viable proof of the existence of UFOs, but was instead meant to whitewash the entire phenomenon. He submits the Air Force's conclusions that 1) no UFO reported, investigated and evaluated by the Air Force was ever an indication of threat to our national security, 2) there was no evidence submitted to or discovered by the Air Force that sightings categorized as "unidentified" represented technological developments or principles beyond the range of modern scientific knowledge, and 3) there was no evidence indicating that sightings categorized as "unidentified" were extraterrestrial vehicles, are simply false.

"The fact that intelligently controlled objects of unknown origin have the capability to neutralize, tamper with, and have control over our most destructive weapons – weapons capable of destroying all living inhabitants on our planet – should be reason enough to demand the disclosure of what has been known to only a small group of individuals," he stated. "The human population deserves the truth."

***

Between January and May 1967, Carl Jennings was a young sailor stationed at a small auxiliary bombing range outside the town of Stumpy Point in Dare County, North Carolina. At the range stood three towers about 100 feet high, where crews would watch as bombers and fighters flew from Seymour Johnson Air Force Base, Naval Air Station Oceana, and several carriers off the coast. Jennings and his fellow sailors were responsible for giving coordinates (triangulating) to determine where the bombs landed. The area was carved from swamps in the shape of a key with one tower at each of the three points. The distance between the towers was approximately one mile. Each tower was manned by at least six individuals, and the main tower is where the night commander, always a senior petty officer, would supervise everyone.

From the main tower looking northward was a gravel road about 20 feet wide that circled the entire swamp, connecting all of the towers and a large storage building on the far north end of the swamp. The area inside the road was all swamp and included a small lake no more than 10 feet deep. Sometime in March, after the first snow of the year, Jennings was in the main tower as the primary observer. Large binoculars were mounted on the steel frame of the tower, which meant Jennings had to actually stand on the outside part of the tower to perform his observations.

"After a break at around 10:45 p.m., I came inside to warm up and immediately grabbed a bottle of soda from the ice chest we always had available," he said. "When I opened the bottle, something caught my eye."

On the north portion of the road, coming from the direction of the storage building, was what appeared to be a military tank, with its treads covering the entire road. It was totally flat on top and had no turret that Jennings could see.

"First, there were no such vehicles on our base," said Jennings. "Second, it glowed a pale bluish-white and was extremely bright. I immediately pointed at the object and called out to everyone to look. Needless to say, we were all in total awe of what we were seeing."

When the object got to the edge of the road, it turned to the east and stopped, slowly hovering over the swamp water, where it changed its shape into an unusual saucer shape. Its wings turned upward, and its tail and nose turned downward. It had no openings, windows or other protrusions other than being very thick in the center, as if it had two or three internal levels.

"It had no markings that I could see, but it did have one heck of a bright white light on the bottom center of it," described Jennings.

"The craft began moving toward the main tower, drifting over the water at maybe 10 feet altitude at best and at about five or 10 miles an hour."

Jennings noted the object was approximately three quarters of a mile from where they first saw it. When it was approximately 100 feet or so from the tower, it turned so the vehicle bottom was facing them and rose to the level of the top of the tower, where the men stood watching in amazement.

"We were all panicky as this 'beast' stared at us," said Jennings, who estimated the craft to have been about 50 to 75 feet in diameter, at least the size of the tower office. It suddenly turned on its light, which practically blinded the sailors, for what seemed like a few minutes. The craft then shut off its light, turned to a level position, and instantly moved to the east tower.

"Its speed was unbelievable; it was almost instantaneous," said Jennings. "It did the same thing over at the east tower and then sped over to the south tower. We all watched and tried to discuss what was happening, but we were totally confused."

According to Jennings, the craft suddenly turned vertical again and took off at an outrageous speed, straight up, disappearing from our line of site within seconds. It took off east directly over the Pamlico Sound towards the Atlantic Ocean. At that point, the phone rang, shocking the men back into reality. It was the senior petty officer, who was livid because he was trying to call since 11 p.m. and nobody would answer the phone. They all looked up at the wall clock, which read 12:50 a.m.

Two hours passed since Jennings first saw the object. How could that be? The men compared wristwatches, and everyone had a different time varying upward of 20 minutes to more than an hour. The commander of the base drove up in a military truck and climbed the stairs to the tower. He was extremely unhappy and cursed the entire crew for their lack of response to the phone calls.

"When we told him what happened, he made a phone call, and within a matter of maybe one minute, four Air Force jets passed over the range with full afterburners heading east towards Pamlico Sound," said Jennings. "We also found out later that two carriers at sea launched fighters after the saucer."

In their minds, it was only a few minutes since the object sped off. The commander ordered the towers closed, and he took the crews from all three towers back to the main barracks, where they were ordered to report to the galley. No one was allowed to leave the room except to use the toilet with an armed guard. Since no military police were assigned to the base, Jennings had no idea where the armed guards came from. In no time at all, there was an entire company of armed MPs blocking the barracks and several other areas. Sitting across the highway about 100 feet from the galley was a large helicopter and two smaller choppers. In all, there were about 20 men who witnessed the event, and they were all sequestered in the galley.

"We sat there from about 1 a.m. until the sun rose, and we weren't allowed to sleep or leave the area," Jennings recalled. "Each of us was called into a room with no windows and interrogated by two men. One was in a suit and never spoke. The other was an Air Force lieutenant colonel. Sometime around 8 a.m., we were all ushered to the helicopters and taken to Seymour Johnson Air Force Base, where we were interrogated as if we were terrorists. We were held totally incommunicado for almost 10 days, at which point I was singled out and sent back to my parent command at NAS Oceana."

Jennings was taken by handcuffs to his barracks to pack his gear and was sent to San Diego in a small business jet with a guard. Once there, he was reassigned to "garbage duty," and a few months later he was shipped off to Vietnam. As a 20-year-old newlywed, this was very hard on Jennings, as he was forced to leave his wife and her family in Virginia. When his wife flew out to see him in San Diego, she could not believe that he was being guarded like a common criminal.

"I was ordered to speak to no one about the incident, not even my wife," said Jennings. "At first she didn't believe me, thinking I was having an affair, which almost led to a divorce. I couldn't tell her that I couldn't talk to her about anything, and that was really difficult on her."

In Vietnam, Jennings was met at his headquarters by two men in business suits who took him aside and warned him in no uncertain terms that, if he made mention of the incident (which was now almost a year ago), he would immediately be transferred to Fort Leavenworth. "Suffice to say, they scared the hell out of me," said Jennings. "Almost 50 years has passed now. I'm close to 70 and in poor health. What's the Navy going to do now? Put me in jail and pay for all my medical care?"

For years, Jennings attempted to sort out and make sense of what happened that night, and he suffered from what he describes as "very strange mental problems" that he could never dare share with a professional. He saw scenes that did not make any sense. There were nights he would go outside in the yard away from his wife and cry like a baby. He had night sweats for years until it finally started to make some sense roughly 30 years after the fact.

"When that object turned on its bright light, something happened to me but I can't explain it," Jennings recalled. "In a dream I had a few weeks after the incident, I remember seeing a room with the brightness of stainless steel. It appeared to be an operating room. I was standing near the table and heard a voice say, 'Not him!' twice. Then I found myself back at the tower. I sat on the floor shaking uncontrollably and then woke up. In the dream, I never saw any occupants. It freaked me out not knowing if it was real or my imagination. Apparently, at least in my dream, I was not accepted by whoever brought me there in the first place. What if I had been accepted? What would have happened to me? Did it happen at all?"

While in Vietnam, Jennings came in contact with a former shipmate who also was on one of the towers. He turned out to be an alcoholic who stayed drunk as often as possible and admitted he was trying to forget what happened that night. He suffered from horrible nightmares and was extremely paranoid.

"We talked for some time until his guard came to take him back to his area," said Jennings. "He mentioned that all the men in

Stumpy Point had been moved out and sent to locations all over the world."

For a long time, Jennings could not help but feel angry about his experience – and more so that he and his mates were treated so poorly by the very institutions they proudly served. He seriously reevaluated how he felt about the military, and he definitely reevaluated how he felt about UFOs and extraterrestrials. He knew that craft could not have been one of ours, or one of the Russians, or anyone else's from this planet. He knew we had nothing that could come close to moving and accelerating the way that object did.

Stumpy Point represents a fascinating case in that dozens of military personnel were not only witness to a UFO, but may have had closer contact with the craft and its occupants then they know, or can fully remember. It also serves as a sad reminder that when military personnel are witness to such events, they are often treated harshly by their superiors, threatened with prison (or sometimes worse) if they talk about the experience, and transferred to far-away locations as if punished for being in the wrong place at the wrong time.

Most significantly, however, what happened at Stumpy Point adversely affected the lives of those who were present that night and caught up in the cover-up storm that quickly followed. Struggling with what they experienced and not allowed to talk to anyone about it, they were forced to deal with it alone, having to shun family members and friends – the people who could have supported them most.

***

Highlighting just some of the other 1967 incidents involving UFOs and the military (missile bases, missile ranges, radar captures, test facilities, naval vessels, fighter jets, war zones, etc.) provides more context and detail as to the nature of these incidents and also shows just how prevalent these incidents were. Many of these reports are documented and available on the NICAP website.

January 7, 1967 — Goose Bay AFB, Labrador, Canada, 11:00–11:05 p.m.: Goose AFB Radar Air Traffic Control (RATCON) radar detected target at 30 miles SW, when target was at 4-6 miles south traveling at very high speed, Goose RATCON notified ADC radar site FPS-93 ground radar operators at the 641at AC&W Squadron, which tracked target at 200 knots (230 mph) then 4 sweeps at 2,100 knots (2,400 mph). Target lost over Goose AFB. Radars on different frequencies. USAF pilot Lt. Col. Gorecki was on approach to runway 27 heading west when he sighted, moving star-like, a steady white light at estimated 5,000 to 7,000 feet overtaking his 160-knot aircraft. Object heading 15 degrees at high speed, disappeared to the north.

February 23, 1967 — Glaskow AFB, Montana: Two separate groups of two personnel each apparently observed the same unidentified object(s). The same apparent object was observed on a MG-13 Fire Control radar. The length of observation was given as two hours.

March 2, 1967 — White Sands Missile Range, New Mexico, 10:25 a.m.–1:30 p.m.: Two radars plotted 20 silver objects, radar blips at 7-mile altitude. News blackout invoked by military. Twenty-nine people reported seeing one or more objects in groups, ranging in appearance from silvery objects flying overhead to a saucer-shaped object. Intermittent unexplained radar targets were seen during this time.

March 5, 1967 — Minot AFB, North Dakota: Air Defense Command radar tracked an unidentified target descending over the Minuteman ICBM missile silos of the 91st Strategic Missile Wing. Base security teams saw a metallic, disc-shaped object with bright flashing lights moving slowly, maneuvering, then stopping and hovering about 500 feet above ground. The object circled directly over the launch control facility. On direct orders from NORAD, F-106 fighters were scrambled, but when this happened the object climbed straight up and disappeared at high speed. It was also reported three armed military teams in trucks pursued the object as it maneuvered and then hovered. The strike teams, who were ordered to capture the craft undamaged if it landed, held their fire and watched as it began moving again, circling directly above a launch control facility.

March 9, 1967 — Las Cruces, New Mexico, 9:30 p.m.: Two administrative staff members of the White Sands Test Facility northeast of Las Cruces saw a fuzzy, fluorescent orange light moving in front of the Organ Mountains to the southeast. It moved toward the witnesses, angled downward, stopped (hovered), then shot straight up and disappeared. Also seen by the wife of the owner of Organ Mountain Lodge, Organ, NM.

March 14, 1967 — Southeast Asia: A U.S. Air Force flight surgeon aboard and the pilot and crew of a KC-135 flying at 15,000 feet observed a vertically inclined, huge, black metallic cylinder an estimated 2 miles from the plane. The object disappeared quickly after several minutes, and fighters sent to investigate could not find it.

March 24, 1967 — Los Alamos, New Mexico (Location of the United States Department of Energy National Laboratory): Disc hovers for 10 minutes.

April 1967 — Brixham, Devon, England: A huge, cone-shaped UFO that slowly revolved, hovered for more than an hour, and shot away as an airplane approached and was seen by members of Her Majesty's Coast Guard and others. Coast Guardsman Brian F. Jenkins stated in his report to the National Investigations Committee on Aerial Phenomena (NICAP) member J. A. Hennessey that the object was seen stationary at approximately 15,000 feet. It slowly drifted to the northwest during the next 80 minutes. It was slowly revolving, revealing a door like structure on its side as it did so. There was a curtain-like structure at its bottom that changed shape during the flight.

April 10-11, 1967 — Houma, Louisiana: Objects were sighted by civilians and Air Force personnel. There were radar returns on MPS-14 and FPS-10 radars. The objects were described as well defined, circular, white, and the size of a dime to a quarter held at arm's length. The radar contact was at 277 degrees at 12 miles and revealed movement from 27,000 to 24,000 feet.

April 17, 1967 — Saigon, Vietnam: Five white oval objects, oriented vertically, moved across the sky in 5 seconds, periodically passing behind small, scattered clouds. Five minutes later jet aircraft at high altitude flew in the same direction as the objects.

May 13, 1967 — Colorado Springs, Colorado (Home to NORAD, Air Force Academy and several other military bases), 4:40 p.m.: At the Colorado Springs airport, an object was picked up on radar. During this time, a Braniff flight was coming in for a landing on runway 35. The track of the object behaved like a ghost echo, perhaps a ground return being reflected from the Braniff aircraft. The object blip appeared at about twice the range of the Braniff blip. When Braniff touched down, however, the situation changed radically. The UFO blip pulled to the right (east) and passed over the airport at an indicated height of about 200 feet. The object track passed within 1.5 miles of the control tower. The object was not visible even through binoculars by personnel in the control tower.

June 3, 1967 — Extremadura, Spain: Two Spanish Air Force fighter pilots chased UFO, radios failed. Cat-and-mouse pursuit. Object shot straight up and disappeared.

June 9, 1967 — Extremadura Province, Spain: Time not reported. A Spanish Air Force jet trainer flying at 1,200 meters altitude encountered an unidentified object that played "cat and mouse" with the plane. The object speeded up and slowed down, and moved above and below the T-33. The aircraft's radio emitted static and ceased to function (electromagnetic effects) when the object was close to the plane. The object finally disappeared climbing vertically at high speed.

June 11, 1967 — Da Nang, Vietnam: Time not reported. An unknown number of witnesses saw a silvery cylinder for several minutes, reportedly chased by two Air Force F-102 interceptors.

July 3, 1967 — Richards-Gebaur AFB, Missouri, 9:30 p.m.: At least seven adults saw a highly reflective disc with three bright orange lights on the rim (body lights) approach from the northeast going on a southerly course. The object had a slight roll and pitch (oscillation) in its forward motion. It was visible for 3-4 minutes until it apparently exploded, dropping fragments to the ground.

August 5, 1967 — Eglin Air Force Base, Florida, 6:40 p.m.: A man saw three whitish oval objects approach Eglin at high speed in a V-formation. They stopped abruptly, hovered over the base at the radar station, and then accelerated out over the Gulf of Mexico. The departure course appeared to follow the path of a radio navigation beam.

September 11, 1967 — Port Elgin, Ontario, Canada, 3:30 p.m.: Six or more employees of a nuclear power plant saw a saucer-shaped object passing over the plant going east. The object hovered about 1.5 miles out over the lake and dropped something into the water. Reportedly, the object returned two nights later and for the next five nights, the assumption being made that it was trying to retrieve the dropped object.

September 11-12, 1967 — Kincheloe AFB, Michigan, 10:42 p.m.-12:01 a.m.: A senior radar operator with seven years experience tracked 17 unknowns in an 80-minute period. The unknown targets gave stronger, harder returns than a B-52 flying in the area. Most of the targets were tracked one at a time, hovering, slowing, speeding up and changing direction. In one of two instances when two were tracked at a time, two targets joined up and both went east at 2,000 mph. These passed overhead, but witnesses saw nothing. A B-52 pilot was alerted to a potential collision course with a target, but the pilot saw nothing.

September 24, 1967 — Minot, North Dakota, 10:30 p.m.: A podiatrist and his wife saw two disc-shaped objects with domes on top. They first appeared as a string of lights flying at high altitude. The string of lights split up and dove below 10,000 feet. Then the two discs separated, one moving away to the north-northeast and the other to the southeast. [Minot AFB Minuteman ICBM Complex]

October 6, 1967 — Vandenberg AFB, California, 7 p.m.: Vandenberg AFB radar detected a very large stationary object some miles over the Pacific off the Northern California coast. Later, radar detected numerous small, but strong, targets traveling eastward in irregular flight.

October 21, 1967 — Blytheville AFB, Arkansas, 6:16 a.m.: Two control tower operators and an observer at the south end of the runway saw two dark oblong table-latter shaped objects with 7-foot-long exhaust at about 1,200-1,500 feet height flying east to west, tracked by RAPCON radar at a distance of 2 miles, made a turn to the southwest then disappeared.

***

When Bill Schroeder tracked several UFOs on his radar screen in B Battery in Key West on March 31, 1967, he had no idea his experience would become part of a massive sighting wave that would have long-term effects on the way many people viewed UFOs. Based on his circumstances, he could not walk into a bar and share UFO experiences with other military personnel, or anyone else for that matter. It was simply too risky, and he could wind up in jail.

The prevailing winds in 1967 dictated that both the United States and Soviet Union be extremely paranoid concerning unexplained activity. Despite the fact these UFOs seemed to function beyond known technological capabilities, both countries must have considered the other one may have developed some type of advanced technology the other did not know about. After all, Operation Paperclip scientists were still working for both sides, focusing on advanced technologies in order to win the Space Race. And what if one of these UFOs crashed in Siberia, or in New Mexico, and some brilliant scientists were able to reverse-engineer that technology? Both the United States and the Soviet Union were well aware of these possibilities, so security surrounding everything UFO-related was critical to the welfare of each nation.

Lord Admiral Hill-Norton was the former UK Chief of Defense Staff, a 5-star Admiral of the Royal Navy, and Chairman of the NATO Military Committee. He was active in the military from WWII until he retired in 1977. Before he died in 2004 at the age of 89, he made the following statement in an interview:

> *Governments believe that if they told the truth, which is that there are objects in our atmosphere, which are technically miles in advance of anything that we can deploy, we have no means of stopping them from coming here, and that we have no defense against them should they be hostile, that I believe is the governments fear if it did disclose those facts. I however, do not believe people would panic. There is a serious possibility that we are being visited and have been visited for many years by other civilizations. Who they are, where they are from and what they want should be the subject of rigorous scientific*

investigation and not the subject of rubbishing by tabloid newspapers.

Paul Hellyer, former Canadian Minister of National Defense, Minister of Transport and member of the Canadian Parliament from 1949 to 1974, shared the following in a 2014 RT News interview:

In one of the cases during the cold war, 1961, there were about 50 UFOs in formation flying south from Russia across Europe. The supreme allied commander was very concerned and was about ready to press the panic button when they turned around and went back over the North Pole. They decided to do an investigation and they investigated for three years, and they decided that with absolute certainty that four different species, at least, have been visiting this planet for thousands of years. There's been a lot more activity in the past two decades, especially since we invented the atomic bomb. They are very concerned about that and if we will use it again, because the whole cosmos is in unity and it affects not just us but other people in the cosmos. They're very much afraid that we might start using atomic weapons again and this would be very bad for us, and for them as well.

The implication here is simple: Governments already know we are visited by extraterrestrial races, but that a) they can do nothing about it, and b) they are determined to keep this information from the general public in fear of starting mass panic.

This policy of secrecy, however, does nothing for the witnesses, who are left alone to struggle with what they see. For civilians, keeping silent is a way to prevent ridicule from friends and neighbors. For military personnel, keeping silent is a way to stay out of jail, or worse. For Schroeder, it would take years for him to finally make inquiries and come forward with his experiences, but by doing so, he presented others with tangible evidence of the existence of UFOs.

The UFO flap of 1967 was significant for many reasons, not the least being the sheer number of sightings people were having worldwide. The fact many of these unidentified craft were tracked by military radar at speeds well beyond any known aircraft's capabilities left many people with much to consider. These radar encounters, captured by trained military personnel, gave credence to many of these sightings, and over the years, as more military personnel have come forward with their stories, it has added fuel to the disclosure fire, because when a body of evidence becomes that massive, it cannot be dismissed by objective observers anymore.

Chapter Eight

Other UFO Incidents Confirmed by Radar

From 1956 to 1960, Gerald Flood served in the United States Air Force as an air traffic control radar operator. In 1958, he was stationed at Eielson Air Force Base outside Fairbanks, Alaska. At the time, Eielson was home to nuclear weapons and high-tech U-2 surveillance technology. The Soviet Union had just boasted its successful launch of Sputnik, the first artificial earth satellite that triggered the Space Race. Sputnik's launch upped the ante in the Cold War and ushered in new political, military, technological, and scientific developments. In 1958, for those who were stationed at U.S. military bases in Alaska, whose far western tip sat only 55 miles from the coast of the Soviet Union, every day was a "high-alert" day.

"Our job was to be ready to attack Russia in case of a nuclear war," said Flood. "This was the purpose of the base ... that and spying on them."

Eielson was built for one purpose. It had a 15,000-foot runway to handle takeoffs and landings from massive, heavy bombers such as the B-36 Peacemakers and the B-47 Stratojets that sat at the ready at all times. Eielson's B-66 Destroyers were constantly on reconnaissance missions, photo-mapping Siberia and the surrounding Russian landscape in order to keep tabs on the nuclear testing the Soviets were engaged in at the time. The base's U-2 spy planes, known as Dragon Ladies, provided high-altitude (70,000 feet) intelligence gathering over Communist territory. It was also used for electronic sensor research, satellite calibration, and communications purposes.

"Those were definitely interesting times," said Flood, who remembers that one of the base pilots was actually shot at while on one of these reconnaissance missions. "Security was so tight at the time that you had to be very careful which zones you flew over because the Soviets would send interceptors up immediately."

Flood's job was to handle surveillance radar and final-approach radar. One night, while on the midnight shift, he was on duty with his crew chief and another radar operator when he noticed a blip on the radar about 30 to 40 miles out from the base. He scanned up to track the target, which was flying at 60,000 feet.

"What the hell is that?" Flood inquired, having heard nothing from the long-range radar operators about any unknown craft in the area. He knew it was not ground clutter because radar had memory, so if an object did not move it would wipe it out on the next sweep.

Suddenly, the object accelerated to 5,000 mph and made a sharp, 90-degree turn. He immediately notified Distant Early Warning (DEW) Line outposts, which knew nothing about the object but also started tracking it once they received the call. He also called nearby Ladd Air Force Base, which tracked the bogey for up to four hours. The object continued to fly at speeds ranging from 3,500 to 5,000 mph, going in circles, suddenly stopping, accelerating again and performing 90-degree right turns.

"The only satellite at the time was Sputnik, and we could see it from the ground, so we knew it wasn't that," said Flood. "Our planes were the best in the world, so I knew there was no plane that could do this, and there was no pilot in the world who could handle those types of maneuvers and speeds."

Ladd AFB decided to scramble a helicopter and a T-33 Shooting Star, a jet trainer aircraft, to get a closer look. At this point, the object was flying directly above Ladd, but the pilots reported only an "ice cloud" over an LAFB energy plant. At around 7:30 a.m., the object suddenly disappeared. Their shift over, Flood and his crew were relieved, but not before all of their log books were confiscated and they were told by their superior officers never to talk about what they had witnessed.

"I never heard another word about it or saw any kind of report," said Flood. "They told us it was a temperature inversion, which just didn't fit at all. That thing was moving all around, and it was too high, and going too fast, and it was picked up on multiple radars. And the right angle turns it was making … no human being could ever have survived that."

Flood, who had top-secret clearance and took an oath of secrecy, had no choice but to keep quiet about what he experienced. "I was a 20-year-old kid who did what he was told," he said. "It did bother me that they dismissed the sighting as a temperature inversion because the radar scope doesn't lie to you. It was great technology, even 50 years ago, and very accurate. There's no way that was temperature inversion."

The "temperature inversion" theory is one many skeptics and debunkers put forth when talking about UFOs being tracked by radar. From a meteorological standpoint, air gets colder as the altitude increases, but under certain conditions there can be layers of warm air with cooler air underneath. These inversions are common in places like the desert, where at night, or when clouds suddenly shadow the hot ground, the surface quickly cools off. Since light moves slower in a denser medium, its rays are refracted, or bent, as they pass from the warm to cold air. This is what causes lake-like mirages on deserts, or the watery sheen you can see when you drive on a hot road. The hot cold layer is refracting light waves from the horizon, and these bent waves are reflecting the sky.

Like light, radar waves move slower in denser medium and are bent by refraction. Under certain conditions, this can be caused when waves strike layers of air with different temperatures. Debunkers say radar observers are merely seeing reflections of ground lights, stars, the moon, or the sun. As such, radar UFOs are simply ground objects picked up by deflected radar beams and shown on scopes as strange blips.

For anyone trained in radar fundamentals, including military radar operators, radar engineers and air traffic controllers, there is a major problem with this theory. When an inversion is big enough, it picks up all kinds of ground clutter, including water tanks, buildings, bridges, shorelines and so on, and anyone who operates a radar recognizes this easily. Both U.S. military and civilian radar experts know enough about temperature inversion to be certain it has nothing to do with the strange objects they track on their scopes.

Additionally, and not least importantly, when it comes to the way a large majority of these events played out, why would military officials (and intimidating men in dark suits who show up shortly after these incidents) confiscate log books and order radar crews never to talk to anyone about what they witnessed if they were simply watching temperature inversions?

In 2005, Flood decided to post his account on a UFO website. Schroeder, who called to hear his story firsthand, noticed his report. "He'd sat on this stuff for 50 years," said Schroeder, "and when I talked to him, he was babbling like a kid who'd just hit a home run."

For Flood, it was an opportunity to validate his experience. For years, he was frustrated by the fact the military treated the sighting with such irreverence. "Bill and I knew we were both well-trained and knew what we were talking about based on our training," explained Flood. "Cases where the recorder is someone trained in radar are important because the evidence is tangible."

Over the years, when Flood heard about UFO sightings, he thought about that night in Alaska almost 50 years ago. "I was happy Bill called," he said. "I'm getting older now, so I want to set the record straight. This thing I tracked, even by today's technological standards, could not have been from this world. You just can't make 90-degree turns like that. The pilot would be killed and the plane destroyed."

***

During the Cold War, Mount Tamalpais, the highest peak in California's Marin Hills, was altered to make way for nuclear missiles. It was one of 28 stations approved by the United States Secretary of Defense on July 21, 1950, as part of the Permanent System Radar Network. Mount Tamalpais Air Force Station was home to the 666th Aircraft Control and Warning Squadron, which was activated on January 1, 1951.

Bob Baker was stationed at the base in 1957-58. He was a radio operator and part of a net control station, a communications station designated to control traffic and enforce circuit discipline within a given net. One night during his time there, he received a message from Navy and Air Force pickets saying they spotted five UFOs heading east towards the Golden Gate Bridge going at speeds higher than anything they had.

"We scrambled three fighter jets out of Hamilton AFB, and we heard one of the pilots freak out because the UFOs turned on a dime and headed back west over the Pacific Ocean," said Baker. "They flew out of sight range very quickly, and you could tell the pilot was distressed over this fact."

He added that, after the incident, he and his crew asked how to log it, but they were told not to log anything, and they had to tell the Navy and Air Force pickets, as well as the Air Force radar planes, the same thing. No one was to log the incident. It never happened.

Baker had another similar experience while manning the radar scope at a military base in Nevada, and the same thing happened afterwards. Headquarters told him not to log a report or tell anyone about the incident.

***

In 1963, Arthur D. Jones was a radar supervisor at Cross City Air Force Station, an Air Defense Command ground interceptor radar site that was part of the Montgomery Air Defense Vector (Southeast Air Defense Vector). This was a unit of the United States Air Force located at Tyndall Air Force Base near Panama City, Florida. The station provided air defense and surveillance for the southeast region of the country.

During one late night shift around 3:30 a.m., Jones got a call from MacDill Air Force Base in Tampa, Florida. The radar supervisor told him they had a stationary target right over Cross City at around 70,000 feet, and it was the second night it had been there.

Jones, wondering why they did not call him the first night to confirm the sighting, called Tyndall AFB and asked if they could take a look as well. They also confirmed the target, so Jones called Patrick Air Force Base in Melbourne, Florida, and asked the same thing.

"I called the weapons officer and told him we had a high-altitude stationary object," Jones recalled. "I got no cooperation from supervision on this, as they didn't seem to know what to do about it."

Several radar sites now had confirmation on the target. Jones and the other radar personnel knew it could not be a weather balloon because with winds at 120 knots at that altitude, there was no way it could remain stationary. They also considered equipment malfunction but quickly realized there was no way that could happen at three radar sites at the same time. A captain who was stationed in the control center felt it was worth checking out, so he told Jones he had two Convair F-106 Delta Dart all-weather interceptors he could scramble. Incapable of reaching 70,000 feet, the captain told the two pilots to climb as high as they could to see what it was.

The interceptors reached Mach 2 pretty quickly, and then one pilot radioed in, "Judy, Judy, Judy," meaning the target was in sight and they were taking control of the intercept. Then he radioed, "Tally Ho, Tally Ho," meaning weapons were locked on the target. When they established lock-on, the object began jamming every radar station in the Southeast. The interceptor pilots panicked and disengaged.

"Everything – all electronics – went blank for about five minutes," said Jones. "When everything returned to normal, the object was gone. I've never experienced anything like that in my life."

Years later, Jones met a retired Air Force officer, who told him he was at the Cross City base that night. The officer said civilians were driving up to the base to tell them there were small objects (spheres) up in the sky darting around a larger stationary object. They were making 90-degree turns at high speeds. Some of the airman at Cross City also saw them.

"Our radar devices were designed to eliminate things that controllers don't need to see, such as ground clutter, rain and objects going less than 120 miles per hour," explained Jones. "So we knew what this thing wasn't, and we had various witnesses, including the captain, the two F-106 pilots, civilians from Cross City, and various radar crews. We all knew there was nothing we had that could come close to doing what this object did."

About a week later, Jones remembers that New Orleans Naval Air Station, Joint Reserve Base, picked up a target meandering over the Gulf of Mexico. They scrambled jets and could not find anything, which left the New Orleans' personnel perplexed. The incident was never officially reported, and the Navy eventually said it was an equipment malfunction.

***

After WWI, both the United States Navy and Army needed means of remotely locating enemy ships and aircraft. In 1930, both services initiated the development of radio equipment to meet this need. The term “radar,” Radio Detection and Ranging, was coined in 1939 by the United States Signal Corps as it worked on these systems for the Navy. After WW II, the Naval Research Laboratory (NRL) and the Army’s Evans Signal Laboratory continued with new activities in centimeter radar development. The United States Air Force – separated from the Army in 1946 – concentrated radar research at their Cambridge Research Center (CRC) at Hanscom Field Air Force Base in Massachusetts. In 1951, MIT opened the Lincoln Laboratory for joint developments with the CRC. While the Bell Telephone Laboratories embarked on major communications upgrades, they continued with the Army in radar for their ongoing Nike air-defense program.

During the Cold War, the primary "axis" of combat shifted to lie between the United States and the Soviet Union. By 1949, both sides had nuclear weapons carried by bombers. To provide early warning of an attack, both deployed huge radar networks of increasing sophistication at ever-more remote locations. In the West, the first such system was the Pinetree Line, a series of radar stations deployed across Canada in the early 1950s and backed up with radar pickets on ships and oil platforms off the east and west coasts.

The Pinetree Line initially used vintage pulsed radars and was soon supplemented with the Mid-Canada Line (MCL). Soviet technology improvements made these Lines inadequate and, in a construction project involving 25,000 people, the Distant Early Warning Line (DEW Line) was completed in 1957. Stretching from Alaska to Baffin Island and covering more than 6,000 miles, the DEW Line consisted of 63 stations with AN/FPS-19 high-power, pulsed, L-Band radars, most augmented by AN/FPS-23 pulse-Doppler systems. The Soviet Unit tested its first ICBM in August 1957, and in a few years, the early-warning role was supplanted almost entirely by the more capable DEW Line.

Both the U.S. and the Soviet Union began to develop major anti-ballistic missile (ABM) systems. In the Soviet Union, radars designated by NATO as the Cat House, Dog House and Hen House supported the Fakel V-1000, which was eventually deployed around Moscow as the A-35 anti-ballistic missile system. In 1957, the U.S. Army initiated an ABM system first called Nike-X. This passed through several names, eventually becoming the Safeguard Program. For this, there was a long-range Perimeter Acquisition Radar (PAR) and a shorter-range, more precise Missile Site Radar (MSR).

The PAR was housed in a 128-foot-high nuclear-hardened building with one face sloping 25 degrees facing north. This contained 6,888 antenna elements separated in transmitting and receiving phased arrays. The L-Band transmitter used 128 long-life traveling-wave tubes (TWTs), having a combined power in the megawatt range. The PAR could detect incoming missiles outside the atmosphere at distances up to 1,800 miles. The MSR had an 80-foot, truncated pyramid structure, with each face holding a phased-array antenna 13 feet in diameter and containing 5,001 array elements used for both transmitting and receiving. Operating in the S-Band, the transmitter used two klystrons functioning in parallel, each with megawatt-level power. The MSR could search for targets from all directions, acquiring them at up to 300 miles range.

Throughout the duration of the Cold War leading up to the present day, radar systems have become more and more sophisticated. Thought-provoking UFO sightings confirmed by radar (both military and civilian) have been documented since the earliest systems were deployed in the 1930s and 1940s.

***

One of the most fascinating UFO radar sightings occurred in 1952 in Washington, D.C. The UFOs were also witnessed by hundreds of people, which makes it one of the most compelling cases of all time. From July 12 through July 29, a series of sightings took place that caused great consternation among both the military and the civilian population because many people believed the nation's capital was being invaded.

On July 19, the sightings came to an apex, when at approximately 11:40 p.m., several unidentified targets were detected on multiple radar screens, including at Washington National Airport and Andrews Air Force Base. The objects moved until they were over prohibited areas such as the White House and the Capitol. Commercial pilots reported seeing white, fast-moving lights, and Andrews AFB reported an orange sphere. When fighter jets were scrambled, the anomalous radar targets disappeared. When the fighters left, the unknowns came back.

These sightings went on intermittently through July 29, when they suddenly stopped. After an official "investigation," the Air Force declared these objects were nothing more than false radar readings caused by temperature inversions. The radar operators were convinced otherwise, and the Air Force apparently failed to take into account the fact these objects were also seen (with the naked eye) by hundreds of eyewitnesses.

***

In 1952, Royal Air Force Flight Sergeant Roland Hughes was returning to his base from a training mission in Germany when he saw a gleaming silver, metallic disc following him. Hughes later described the disc as shiny, like tin foil, without a single crease of crinkle, and about the size of an Avro Lancaster bomber. The object descended and began traveling alongside him before flying off at an incredible speed. Royal Air Force radars tracked the object, and controllers confirmed that the object traveled at speeds way beyond what any aircraft were capable of at the time.

Six days later, Hughes was sent to West Germany to give his official account of what happened to several senior RAF officers and Duncan Sandys, the British Minister of Aviation. Sandys was so taken by Hughes' story that he briefed senior civil servants on the matter, telling them he was convinced it was true. Hughes never spoke about the incident unless prompted by his family.

***

In August 1956, the night-watch supervisor at the Lakenheath Radar Air Traffic Control Center in England was stunned by a telephone call from the Bentwaters Ground Control Approach radar installation.

"Do you have any targets on your scopes traveling at 4,000 mph?"

The objects in question were performing amazing aerobatic feats way beyond the capabilities of any known aircraft. The radar images were corroborated by both air and ground sightings. A pilot in a C-47 saw one of these objects pass directly underneath his plane. The night-watch supervisor informed the Royal Air Force Station at Wimbledon, which in turn scrambled fighter jets to intercept.

Military personnel watched their radar screens as an interceptor pilot tried to engage one of the objects from behind, before getting outmaneuvered with the object ending up behind him. The pilot was unable to shake the target off his tail and requested assistance. A second interceptor pilot asked: "Did you see anything?"

"I saw something, but I'll be damned if I know what it was," the first pilot said.

"What happened?" asked the second pilot.

"He – or it – got behind me, and I did everything I could to get behind him and I couldn't. It's the damnedest thing I've ever seen."

The first pilot, who reportedly sounded pretty scared, said that he was returning to base because he was running low on fuel. The second pilot, before he could get close enough to pick up anything, radioed that he was experiencing engine malfunction and returned to base.

***

In December 1978, in the Kaikoura Mountain Ranges of New Zealand, a series of radar and visual UFO sightings remains one of the world's best documented UFO cases. On December 20, an Argosy freight plane flight crew observed strange lights around their aircraft. The objects, which appeared to be tracking them, were picked up by air traffic control in Wellington and Christchurch as well as the aircraft's on-board radar. A television crew from Australia, hired to film a reenactment of the December 20 incident, actually saw and filmed the UFOs on December 30 while on an Argosy freight plane. Once again, the objects were tracked by radar in both Christchurch and Wellington. A massive, bright, orb-like object was also filmed by the television crew, observed for several minutes, and tracked by radar.

After the sightings, the Royal New Zealand Air Force, local police and Carter Observatory joined forces in an investigation. The Ministry of Defense claimed the lights were unburned meteors, squid boat lights, the planet Venus, or harbor lights. Obviously, these somewhat obtuse explanations did not sit well with the witnesses.

"None of them to my knowledge of satisfaction have coordinated the visual sighting with the radar sighting," said Bill Startup, the pilot of the Argosy on the night of December 30. "You name it, they can come up with all sorts of reasons for what it was, but they haven't explained how I can see Jupiter, Venus, and the harbor lights doing 140 knots on my radar."

***

Captain Kenju Terauchi is etched into Ufology lore due to an incident on November 17, 1986 that occurred while he was piloting

Japan Air Lines cargo flight 1628. Terauchi, an ex-fighter pilot with more than 10,000 hours of flight experience, was flying over Alaska, en route from Paris to Narita International Airport in Tokyo, when the crew first witnessed two unidentified objects to their left. The two mysterious objects followed the plane so closely the crew could feel the warmth of their lights on their faces. A third, larger object arrived just as the two smaller objects sped away.

At this point, Terauchi radioed Anchorage Air Traffic Control and requested a change of course. Anchorage controllers also picked up the objects on radar and gave the crew a directive to evade the unidentified crafts, but no matter how many turns or drops Terauchi made, the object continue to follow them for 400 miles.

After the incident, Federal Aviation Administration (FAA) officials interviewed the crew and determined they were all rational, normal and professional. Terauchi cited in the official FAA report that the object was a UFO, and when later he gave an interview with two Kyodo News journalists telling them the same thing, Japanese Air Lines grounded him and reassigned him to a desk job.

Three months later, after the FAA presented the data to representatives of the FBI, CIA, and President Ronald Reagan's Scientific Study Team, it retracted earlier suggestions that their controllers had confirmed UFOs, and they concluded the sighting was the result of a "split radar image" that appeared with "unfortunate timing." Once again, they failed to even account for the fact that Terauchi and his crew were in visual contact with these unidentified craft for more than 400 miles.

Here is an excerpt from communication between Japan Air Lines flight 1628 (JAL) and Anchorage Air Traffic Control (ATC):

JAL: Anchorage Center. Japan Air 1628, ah, do you have any traffic, ah, seven o'clock above?

ATC: JAL1628 heavy, say again …

JAL: Do you have any traffic in front of us?

ATC: JAL1628 heavy, roger.

JAL: Ah, roger and, ah, we in sight, ah, two traffic, ah, in front of us one mile about.

ATC: JAL1628, roger, do you have …, ah, can you identify the aircraft?

JAL: Ah, we are not sure, but we have traffic in sight now.

ATC: JAL1628 heavy, roger. Maintain visual contact with your traffic and, ah, can you say the altitude of the traffic?

JAL: Uh, almost the same altitude.

ATC: JAL1628 roger. Would you like a higher or lower altitude?

JAL: Ah, no, negative.

ATC: JAL1628 heavy, see if you are able to identify the type of aircraft, ah, and see if you can tell whether it's military or civilian.

JAL: We cannot identify the type, ah, but we can see, ah, navigation lights and ah, strobe lights.

ATC: Roger, sir. Say the color of the strobe and beacon lights.

JAL: The color is, ah, white and yellow, I think.

ATC: White and yellow. Thank you.

John Callahan, a former head of the FAA's Accidents, Evaluations and Investigations Division in the 1980s, was ordered to attend the FAA meeting with the CIA, FBI, and the President's scientific staff after the Japan Air Lines incident.

In a 2012 interview with the Huffington Post, he said he had to hand over all information, including radar reports, about the case to them. "After I showed them the materials three times, one of them stepped forward and said, 'This event never happened. We were never here. We're confiscating all this data, and you're all sworn to secrecy.'"

Callahan then asked a CIA agent if it would be okay to contact the media about the UFO incident, and he was told, "You can't do that. It would frighten the American public. They can't know about this."

When asked by the Huffington Post if he believed the earth is being visited by extraterrestrials, Callahan replied, "Oh, I think we really are, and the government doesn't tell you the truth all the time. Part of the stuff I was doing in my last 10 years with the government was lying to the public. I gave out disinformation – an approved tactic by the government – because the people can't handle the truth."

***

The Belgian UFO wave began in November 1989 and lasted for several months. The wave would be documented (both visually and by radar) by thousands of civilians, various groups of police officers, military radar operators and F-16 pilots. On March 30,

1990, after having received various reports of unusual lights as bright as stars that changed color, the Control & Reporting Center (CRC) at Glons confirmed on radar that a giant triangular object was in the skies above Belgium. Soon after, a second set of lights was sighted moving towards the first triangular craft, and after receiving a second radar confirmation, two F-16 jets were scrambled from Beauvechain Air Base to intercept.

The F-16s attempted to intercept the bogey nine times, but every time they obtained radar lock, the object changed its position or accelerated so fast that the locks were broken. During the first radar lock, the object accelerated from 150 mph to more than 1,100 mph while changing altitude from 9,000 feet to 5,000 feet and back up to 11,000 feet in less than two seconds. During this encounter, more than 13,000 people witnessed the unfolding drama from the ground. After a little more than an hour, the object disappeared from the various radar screens and the F-16's returned to base.

***

In March 2004, a Mexican Air Force Merlin C26A bi-motor airplane was performing routine duties to detect drug smuggling airplanes in an anti-narcotics operation in and around the city of Campeche. The plane had a high-tech FLIR STAR ZAPPHIR II and a RADAR AN/PS 143 BRAVO VICTOR 3, which implements infrared video. At around 5 p.m., the crew detected an unknown craft at 10,500 feet. The plane flew closer to get visual confirmation, but when it did, the object made a surprise maneuver and flew away at great speed. The entire event was being recorded, and the details were being reported as they occurred to base. Without warning, the unknown object suddenly reappeared and began following the Merlin.

The crew now saw two objects on radar, but there was still no visual contact. The crew could not maneuver to enable a visual confirmation of the unknown objects, and they became alarmed. Within the next few minutes, nine more objects surrounded them. Though close enough to see the unknowns, the crew stated the objects must have been invisible. Suddenly the 11 UFOs were gone. The Merlin and her crew returned to the Air Force base, baffled, bewildered and shaken.

The good news is the Mexican government released all radar and infrared footage and gave the worldwide media access to the crew and the head of the Mexican Air Force. “Was I afraid? Yes,” said radar operator Lt. German Marin. “A little afraid because we were facing something that had never happened before.”

Chapter Nine

Radar Data as Tangible Evidence of UFOs

When it comes to paranormal phenomena, collecting tangible evidence is the key to providing authenticity to witness accounts. Whether it's a UFO, ghost or Bigfoot sighting, being able to capture a photograph, a sound recording or a radar signature goes a long way in not only convincing others the incident really occurred. However, much more importantly, it provides researchers and scientists with evidence they need to perhaps answer why and how these phenomena occur.

As it relates to UFOs, when reports of reversals, sharp turns, rapid climbs and descents are fully confirmed, no natural phenomena can explain that, and the swift acceleration of these craft far exceeds the acceleration of man-made rockets and guided missiles. No earthly craft can reverse from high speed or make the violent turns proved by radar tracks. Additionally, radar acquisitions are usually made by trained observers, which, backed up by tangible echo returns becomes harder to deny. The fact that naked-eye observers corroborate many of these radar visuals adds even further credence to their authenticity.

Donald E. Keyhoe, a former Marine Corps naval aviator, UFO researcher and co-founder of NICAP, always argued that the U.S. government should conduct appropriate research into UFO matters and release all its UFO files to the general public. He researched and wrote extensively on the topic of UFOs and was highly regarded as a leader in the field of Ufology.

In 1952, he wrote the following in an article for *True, The Man's Magazine*:

"The increasing evidence from the radar-and-ground reports cannot be denied. It is my opinion, as previously stated in True, that the saucers are devices from outer space, exploring the earth just as our government expects some day to explore other planets."

It is difficult to comprehend the significance of UFOs tracked on radar (and in many cases, military jets scrambled to intercept them) unless you also take into account the fact thousands of these cases have been documented, and several more thousand have probably been swept under the rug. In one year alone, 1952, the director of Air Force Intelligence admitted more than 300 cases of radar tracking and visual sightings confirmed by radar. In the ensuing years leading up to 1967, when Schroeder and Force had their encounters, there were at least 2,000 additional radar cases in the United States alone.

That was 50 years ago, which suggests that by now, in the year 2016, there have been tens of thousands of cases of radar tracking and visual sightings confirmed by radar. Reports have come from expert operators in the Army, Navy, Air Force, Marine Corps, Coast Guard, the Federal Aviation Agency (as it was known at the time), and pilots or radar operators of all the major airlines. The same applies to foreign countries, which have been either more or less apt to share this information with the rest of the world.

Keyhoe went on to say "not only has radar proved UFO reality, it has accurately recorded the high UFO speeds, intricate maneuvers, precise formations – including changes from one formation to another – and other important data which make it possible to evaluate UFO operations and help in the search for propulsion secrets. ... When the full story of the UFOs is written, radar will prove to have supplied indisputable technical evidence which finally convinced many previous skeptics."

Robert Salas, who was witness to the Malmstrom AFB incident in 1967, refers to another case in 1957, when Major Lewis Chase and his crew were flying a specially equipped reconnaissance RB47 over the Gulf of Mexico and encountered a UFO approaching them at high speed. The UFO was seen by crew members, and it demonstrated the ability to stop instantly and seem to appear and disappear at will. It followed the aircraft through a two-hour mission. It was tracked over the southwest United States by airborne radar and ground radar. When the RB47 landed, members of AFOSI met the crew and confiscated all the recorded data and photographs. This incident was documented in SECRET Blue Book files.

"Radar data is tangible evidence because it records the speed and maneuverability of these craft that far exceeds any we humans can manufacture," said Salas.

He also refers to the 1986 incident involving Japan Air Lines flight 1628 as a perfect example of how tangible, corroborate evidence is documented. Unfortunately, it also represents one of the many cases where the evidence was confiscated by government officials and the media refused to look into why this happened. As noted earlier, former FAA Official John Callahan has been very vocal about the government's "disinformation" policy regarding UFOs.

"Callahan detailed this incident publicly in 2001, over 15 years ago, and I have spoken of and written about the RB47 incident over five years ago," explained Salas. "That tells you something about the media bias against fully investigating and acknowledging this very tangible evidence. It also highlights the fact that the valid and best evidence is available but being held by government agencies in secrecy and counter to the public right to know the truth about this phenomenon."

Schroeder, who knew from the moment he tracked his "bogeys" that he was witnessing something extraordinary and possibly not of this earth, was excited that they were also tracking these objects at Homestead AFB. Certainly this was going to be huge national news, and a joint investigation would be forthcoming from the U.S. military and several government agencies. Perhaps there was an investigation, but the American people never heard about it, and the witnesses themselves were never told anything. Instead, they were simply stripped of their evidence, told to keep quiet, and separated by being shipped off to various military posts around the world. Again, at the time, Schroeder was only a kid doing his duty, and he was more concerned about staying out of trouble than alerting the world to his experiences. Over time, however, not being able to share a story with implications that would change the course of human history becomes both a heavy burden and a frustrating struggle between military loyalty and the truth.

"I kept my mouth shut for the most part, but every once in a while, I did talk to Dennis about it," said Schroeder. "I was digging into this case, and learning more about the UFO phenomenon in general, for years before I was out of public service and able to go public with my story."

Chase Kloetzke has investigated UFOs, strange creatures, and the paranormal for more than 20 years. She is a former deputy director of investigations and Star Team manager for the Mutual UFO Network (MUFON), the largest civilian UFO investigative organization in the United States. In addition, she has trained U.S. military personnel as a master trainer and master instructor, having designed and taught specialized programs relating to Force Readiness and Elite Force Protection. She has investigated several UFO cases involving radar tracking and visual sightings confirmed by radar. Kloetzke admits that absolute truth is often illusive, but this does not mean you should stop searching for it.

"Tangible, physical or trace evidence is the Holy Grail of any UFO investigation, as it offers admissibility and a great chance to meet a burden of proof," she explained. "This burden is the responsibility of each investigator, as scrutiny will inevitably follow any and all claims. Physical evidence does not have bias and is often 'testable,' as it narrows down the possibilities, including speculation. It's an independent component to any event."

Radar signatures of UFOs going at ridiculous speeds and performing impossible maneuvers, in particular, are important to UFO research because of the extraordinary nature of the tracking.

"Radar reports are very important to UFO cases because they are a 'technical eyewitness' to something in our airspace that is not known to the controller," she continued. "They are tracked, recorded, documented and analyzed, as they are considered first a safety hazard in our sky, but also a National Security risk. These returns are often taken seriously and treated with the best attention in the control towers."

The fact military radar operators and air traffic controllers witness these types of incidents makes the evidence even more credible because these individuals are trained to observe situations and eliminate what they are not. According to Kloetzke, when adding the highly trained observer's testimony to an echo return or radar report, from those seated at a radar panel during an unknown intrusion sighting, there is an undeniable strength to the sighting and report.

"Other observers – such as a pilot who has a visual on a craft, or a ground observer – represent corroboration and are considered high-value evidence," she said. "Military Air Traffic Controllers are skilled and trained observers. Radar can and has been susceptible to errors and anomalies, but training includes identification protocol that leaves little to no questions regarding whether an event was a physical object vs. atmospheric anomalies. The military can quickly gain other sources of expert attention such as climatologists or astronomical-type personnel. Expert corroboration is, in fact, hard to dismiss or deny."

Kloetzke places enormous significance on the fact UFOs are often tracked over missile bases because, according to her, frequency indicates interest and intent. "These are undeniable no-fly zones and heavily monitored for safety and intrusions. There would be no reason, without a battery of permissions, to have any craft, plane or air operated devices over a military base or nuclear site," she stressed. "These would clearly be violations of 'Arial Off Limit Areas.' Usually, there are strict penalties for intrusions, including shoot-down orders. When unknown craft violate this air space, especially more than once, it's a clear and realistic National Security risk that would receive the highest attention."

When their incidents occurred, Schroeder was on duty as a fire control operator at an Army Air Defense HAWK missile battery; Force was at his radar post near Homestead Air Force Base, home to a tactical fighter squadron; and Salas was on duty as a Deputy

Missile Combat Crew Commander (DMCCC) at a Minuteman Launch Control Facility. This is no coincidence. Frequency indicates interest and intent. These UFOs were there not only because they were interested in our military capabilities, but they also had intent.

In the South Florida incident, the UFOs seemed to be searching for something. At Malmstrom, they clearly effected missile operations. At military bases around the world, these same scenarios have played out for decades, and although fighter jets sent to intercept these objects seemingly never do, we are at least left with the radar tracking as tangible, quantifiable evidence that cannot be ignored.

Chapter Ten

Military Personnel as UFO Witnesses

I have kept this secret for decades and do not wish to go to my grave with the things that we all witnessed in Cuba. I was a marine stationed at Guantanamo Bay in the late 1960s. I mostly worked fence duty as part of the security forces there. I remember the first time I saw what could only be described as a UFO. I was amazed and didn't expect to see anything like it again. But I did. We all did.

There were things going on every night it seemed. Some of these lights would fly overhead less than 300 feet! Most of what we saw were lights, but they were surrounded by a cloud-like substance or a haze. You know, like what you see on very hot days. I did have a memory recently that once or twice I could make out a boomerang shape. Most of the sightings had to have been large craft because of the cloud/haze around the lights, which, I can't verify, were always connected with just one craft every time. Most were no less than 50 feet to no more than 100 feet across. It's difficult to identify the exact size even while seeing it. There seemed to be a small red light trailing them most times, too, and that's how we knew that it was the end of the sighting. These objects were seen while we were working perimeter duty or the fence line of the base.

One night, I was on guard duty at the main gate. This is where most traffic in and out would be. It was about 7 p.m. and dark at this time, and I stepped out of the guard shack and looked outside of the gate to the Cuban guard house and saw immediately a white, cloud-like, hazy formation with blueish white lights, or a baby blue color if you will, pulsating in the middle of this cloud substance. I asked the other marine guard with me if he saw this, too. It was now rising up over the Cuban guard shack and moving towards our position.

Just then, we heard an urgent call from our marine sergeant in the watch/observation tower yelling for us to get the hell out of there! It was too late, as this cloud was directly over us at this time, and we didn't move. It was completely silent. We heard nothing. I believe we stood there for several minutes before hearing the sergeant from the tower ordering us to pull back and leave the shack. Basically, to abandon a strategic post and head back to our barracks. This was also a very strange order.

The barracks were about 200 feet away on a hill, and I remember quite clearly seeing a crew of Base Intelligence personnel now filming this object. I saw them film for about 3 hours … 3 solid hours! Then the cloud with the lights starting moving down the fence line in a western direction. After what appeared to be about 1/4 mile, the object stopped and shot straight up like a bullet until we couldn't see it anymore.

On the south side of the island at another guard post, we also witnessed many, many times UFOs coming into and out of the ocean. These were mostly blue or whitish lights and large. Again, it would be hard for me to put an exact size on them, but they would move around while out of the water. When they would re-enter the ocean, they appeared to slow down and dim, which I knew was the result of them descending. We would watch these for an hour or two. Sometimes a saucer shape would be seen, but these were quick. I know for a fact that we were well aware of them. We witnessed jets chasing them over the ocean.

I was never frightened by what I witnessed and quite frankly enjoyed seeing them. I was fascinated more than anything, but some [of the other men] were frightened by what they saw. We were never offered a brief or explanation, and I talked with many marines about the events throughout my tour of 13 months. This was something known to be happening on this base at least during 1968 and 1969.

Before my transfer was completed, I was brought to headquarters on base and a major sat me down and told me to not talk about what I saw, and I did sign a secrecy document that lasted 10 years. I decided to come forward now because I'm 70 years old and do not wish to keep this secret with me. Those 10 years are long gone.

Guantanamo Bay NE Gate 1968

***

UFO and paranormal researcher Chase Kloetzke, who recently conducted a thorough investigation of the Guantanamo Bay case and documented the above witness testimony, always finds one common denominator when researching UFO cases involving military personnel. According to her, the "thin red line," or the strong camaraderie between service men and women, is absolutely a reality.

"Military servicemen and woman stick together and are usually most at ease around their own. This also includes the military veteran that will often join veteran organizations," she explained. "Vets will talk with and be more open with other vets; it's just the way it is. It also never matters when, where or how you served, just that you wore the uniform. It is my experience that most military members will talk about something they have witnessed long after they believe their secrecy agreement has expired or the event has been declassified. They sometimes struggle with secrecy and the feelings that the public has a right to know, or they understand that they have witnessed something they view as NOT in their contracts, so to speak. And if it's so anomalous, why is it covered up?"

Kloetzke believes most military personnel have a strong sense of national security, honor and commitment. There are times when an incident or situation will test the member and cause a conflict in truth and duty. If a military member has many years of service or retirement status, they will most likely experience this conflict a few times.

"This would be the worst-case scenario for any military member since they are under secrecy agreements and security identifications such as 'classified' or 'top secret,'" she added. "To violate any classified information is met with heavily enforced penalties, such as long prison terms or separation under less than honorable circumstances. The 'less than honorable' carries a stigma that lasts a lifetime and causes detrimental reactions from employers to neighbors. It's a distinction that most will not risk carrying."

***

When human beings experience something extraordinary, or beyond their current understanding of what is real or possible, everything changes for them. They often undergo what is referred to as a personal paradigm shift, where a major "re-evaluation" occurs regarding the framework of their basic assumptions, ways of thinking and belief systems. In science, a paradigm shift refers to a major change in a cognitive framework or methodology that are commonly accepted by members of a scientific community.

After witnessing a UFO, for example, one might reconsider whether or not we are alone in the universe. When a person sees a ghost, they may begin to question what happens when we die. For open-minded individuals who believe in all possibilities, having such experiences represents a validation of what they always thought was possible in the first place. But for most people, who are indoctrinated at young ages by religious dogma and other institutional teachings, things are often black and white with absolutely no room for any detours or bumps in the road.

Today, things are slowly changing as people wake up both spiritually and intellectually to all possibilities. They tend to be more critical of old institutions that are either failing them or not providing the same sense of security they once did. In the 1950s and 1960s, however, many Americans were very loyal to the institutions their parents and grandparents swore to; whether you were a "good Christian" or a "true patriot," these things mattered a great deal to the social underpinnings of American culture. It was not until the late 1960s that a subculture grew, made up of mostly the younger generation, who was distrustful of the U.S. government and authority in general.

When you saw a UFO in the 1940s, or '50s, or '60s, you were stuck with a major dilemma for two reasons. First, you were most likely distressed by what you saw, and second, you dare not have told anyone in fear of being ridiculed and shunned socially. If you were in the military, you had a third dilemma: You were ordered not to talk about this incident, and if you did, you ended up in prison. Such was the plight of many military personnel who were witnessing events associated with these major UFO waves that hit the United States, and the world, during this time period.

Bill Schroeder has always been open-minded and objective. But even for him, his experience was paradigm-shifting. "It changed my life instantaneously because I realized that what we were experiencing was other-worldly and that we were now in on the biggest secret in the history of history," he said. "This is the story of mankind, the story of who we are and where we're going. And to be given this knowledge, or awareness if you will, at the age of 17 was amazing. I tell everybody that while everyone else was running around with their hair on fire and panicking that night, I just looked up into the sky with a huge smile on my face because I realized I was in on the biggest secret there is, or the greatest story that's never been told."

From that moment forward, Schroeder has looked up to the sky, looking for things most people do not looking for. "Since that night, I've always looked for them, but they never came back, to my knowledge," he said. "That bugs me a bit, but I'm never going to stop looking."

After the incident, Schroeder went into law enforcement and his cousin Dennis went into state investigation, so neither could talk about it for years. Over the years, Schroeder did speak to a few select law enforcement officers who he really trusted. One of these men, Mark McAllister, first met Schroeder in Tennessee in 1982, when Schroeder took a break from law enforcement and was a chief at a security company. They worked together there and again in the late 1980s in the police force, where Schroeder was chief and McAllister was a sergeant.

"Bill brought the incident up to me while we were riding together one day in 1985," recalled McAllister. "He would always talk about astronomy and the universe, as well as his time in the military. He also mentioned UFOs and his interest in them, and then one night, he told me about his experience at B Battery. He told me about the blips on the radar screen, these bogeys moving at speeds nobody could match, and how they would disappear moving vertically like a rocket."

At first, McAllister was surprised, and it struck him as unusual but not unbelievable. When you work in law enforcement, you learn to expect anything, and he had great respect for Schroeder, so he believed his story.

"Bill is very passionate, and you can tell when somebody is serious and truthful about something," said McAllister. "After talking to him about it, I knew it was real, and we talked about it several times afterwards. Bill was frustrated because nobody in the military wanted to talk about it, and he always wanted to know what those things were. When your superiors tell you to forget about something as shocking as what he witnessed, you start to wonder."

McAllister also believes the time period in question played a major factor in why this incident was extraordinary. "This was a few years removed from the Cuban Missile Crisis," he stated, "so for something like this to happen, and for your commanding officers to dismiss it is significant."

He also knew this meant a great deal to Schroeder. "I studied aviation, so I wasn't as shocked and disbelieving as others might have been," he says. "It wasn't the first time I had heard a story like that, and I thought it was definitely possible we were being visited by extraterrestrials, and that their technology might allow for those types of maneuvers."

The biggest factor for McAllister was the source of the story. "Bill is someone I trust implicitly," he said. "He's like a brother to me, and he is one of the most honest, upstanding people I've ever known. If he says something happened, it happened. I just felt bad because you could tell he was frustrated by the whole thing, and at that time, he couldn't get anyone else to talk about stuff like that."

Schroeder's cousin Force felt the same frustration. "Bill and I talked about it a lot, but not to anyone else," he said. "The military didn't realize we were cousins, and they never made the connection. They probably always thought we didn't even know each other."

Force stressed they were sworn to secrecy, and the military drummed that into your head as you went through tech school. Force's crypto training was top secret, as were the things he was trained to decipher. When you had top-secret clearances, you did not mess with that sworn oath to secrecy. "I wasn't about to go on TV and tell the world about what we witnessed that night. It did bother me a lot that the only person I could really talk to about it was Bill, but over time, I realized it wasn't a NORAD exercise and that these things weren't conventional aircraft. Quite frankly, we didn't have anything that came close to traveling at 5,000 miles per hour."

As far as closure is concerned, Force believes it will only come if there is disclosure. "We know what we experienced, but it's frustrating that it all gets covered up and dismissed as nonsense," he said. "Not only is it not nonsense, but it is the most important phenomenon to occur in human history."

As faithful military men, Force and Schroeder did what they had to do by keeping quiet for many years. "If you take it to your grave, that is a tough burden to bear, so I think, as human beings, we have to search for the truth," said Force. "Bill and I eventually did that, and it has been very freeing for us. When you're 20 years old and in the military, you don't question things, especially when they tell you not to or you will go to Leavenworth. But over time, you start to resent being told not to talk about something so profound; we knew the significance of these events to mankind."

Salas understands firsthand what Schroeder and Force went through. He endured the same thing regarding the Malmstrom AFB incident and also eventually came forward after years of silence. He believes that, in the military, it is very difficult because of the need to maintain secrecy.

"The command and control structure is such that all officers and men are obliged to carry out orders and follow regulations. This is especially true in nuclear missile units where everyone deals with many classified documents," said Salas. "Commanders have the ability to classify any activity. In addition, classified information is generally compartmentalized on a need-to-know basis. It is very difficult to know if something significant has occurred, and incidents can easily be covered up."

Salas eventually came out to discuss his case publicly, but he had to weigh the importance of the information against what he perceived to be the true national security impact of revealing information versus the public interest in knowing the information. He had to keep in mind the U.S. government has the right and the responsibility to maintain secrecy in matters of national security, and it also has final say as to what to classify and how high the classification is. In his case, Salas always believed the public interest outweighed the so-called national security impact, but he also had to consider his legal obligation to maintain secrecy and the consequences of releasing it.

"In some cases, witnesses were only verbally cautioned not to release the information or were not told not to reveal it. In those instances, there is little risk in coming forward. In other cases, as in mine, there were written non-disclosure statements, which I had to sign," he explained. "This is a legally binding statement, and I certainly could be prosecuted for revealing the information related to my incident. At first, I thought I was in the clear when, in 1994, I received documents under FOIA for the Echo Flight incident. Two years later, when I realized I had not been at Echo but at Oscar Flight, I knew I was at risk of being prosecuted. However, I decided to continue speaking about my incident because of its significance for the public interest. I took a calculated risk based on the scenario that, if I was prosecuted, I would 'blow the whistle' even louder and the government would have much to answer for on UFOs. That tactic seems to have worked because I've been outspoken about it for over 20 years, and I have never been approached by anyone in government to cease and desist."

In Schroeder's case, he never signed a non-disclosure statement, but he still had to consider the impact coming forward could have on his personal life. His decision to go into law enforcement precluded him from becoming a "whistleblower" at the time because his career would have been impacted in a negative way. "And I was still very young," he added. "I had my whole life ahead of me and didn't want to jeopardize my livelihood. As I got older, however, I had less to lose."

Both Schroeder and Salas, as well as most people in this country, realize that they have little to no power in relation to the U.S. military or government. Stories abound regarding whistle blowers and how their lives were ruined as a result of coming forward, especially in matters concerning UFOs. Then there is the theory that the U.S. government and other unknown forces have been murdering UFO researchers and whistleblowers, with some claiming a death toll as high as several dozen or even more.

Whether or not this is true, the UFO phenomenon is a high-stakes matter, and the secrecy and intimidation tactics employed by military and government agencies validates the notion that not only are they real, but whoever is flying these craft are not from this planet. Having said this, if you are bound by national security, yet you decide to come forward with information you believe is important to the general public, you do so at your own risk.

If a witness wants to come forward, Salas suggests they do the following:

- If possible, acquire documentation to corroborate your claim.
- Enlist the commitment of witnesses to back you up.
- Discuss your intentions with someone you trust, and if possible another "whistleblower." (Salas said he would be available for this role, or he could also suggest other ex-military who have come forward.)
- Develop a plan for your release of information. Again, it would be helpful to have support of others at the time of your announcement.
- Carefully write down the specific information you are releasing and review it carefully; allow a trusted friend to read it, then re-write it for clarity before making your announcement.

- Anticipate possible outcomes from your announcement. In particular, consider the real possibility that what you release will be disputed, denied and/or ridiculed.
- Be available and prepared to answer any and all questions related to your disclosure. Once you are "out," be as vocal as you can be.
- If possible, arrange for media (post announcement) interviews prior to your announcement.

When Schroeder came out with his story, he was approached as a military witness by UFO researcher Linda Molton Howe, and days later he was talking about it with her on a popular, syndicated radio show. After that, Schroeder became active in both NICAP and MUFON, and as a result, they started to pay closer attention to what happened and further researched the incident. To Schroeder, he is serving his country even more so now.

"Men my age, part of NORAD and the old air defense sectors, there are probably thousands of us left who have tracked UFOs, and it's time to step forward and do a final duty for your country," he stressed. "Step forward and let the truth out. We owe it to the Americans we served and we owe it to ourselves. To be able to step out of the shadows and say, hey, this is what was happening, and you have a right to know. My goodness, we were serving the people of the United States of America, and it's time to serve these people again with the truth."

Afterword

This book is the result of one man's courage and conviction to come forward with his amazing story. If Bill Schroeder decided to take his secret to the grave, very few people would ever have heard about "the night" and the incredible details surrounding a potentially disastrous Cold War incident that should have made headlines at the time. Schroeder did come forward, and I was fortunate enough to meet his cousin Dennis at a UFO conference. He, in turn, was gracious enough to tell me his part of the story and get me in contact with Schroeder.

When thinking about the purpose of this book, I spoke with Schroeder and concluded that this story simply needed to be shared. I also believed that by sharing the stories of other military witnesses and radar operators, readers would develop a clearer picture as to the magnitude of these incidents. The importance of radar as tangible evidence of UFOs, the struggle of military personnel who are sworn to secrecy, and the intent of these UFOs to check out missile bases, not only in the United States but around the world, cannot be overstated enough.

As a whole and corroborative set of evidence, these incidents may possibly represent the most important story ever told. The stakes to humanity cannot be higher. If we are indeed being visited by extraterrestrial life forms, why are they here, and what do we need to learn as a rather primitive and violent race in order to evolve and become part of whatever galactic collective exists? Are we meant to join our friends out there in peace and understanding, or are we meant to destroy ourselves before we get the chance?

From the beginning, one thing I wanted to establish was what Schroeder and Force thought actually happened that night, especially after they had a chance to piece more information together. Schroeder has a sound theory:

"Recently, I've accepted the fact that, based on the incidents in Puerto Rico and at Crestview Elementary School – and based on the fact that the UFOs didn't seem to care if we knew they were there and flying a grid pattern and search pattern – they lost one of their own, and they were doing the same exact thing we would do if we lost one of our own: get there as fast as possible and do a thorough job," he explained. "Realize, they came to South Florida at a very high rate of speed, and once they got here, they slowed down and started to perform a grid search. Over and over again. They were looking for something, and looking back, I hope they eventually found it, maybe in the Everglades or somewhere in the Atlantic Ocean. Based on the way they were moving that night, they had an agenda, and they were not going to be stopped from doing what they had to do."

Force agrees. "Both sets of four bogeys were definitely in a search pattern, the same way the Coast Guard does it," he said. "I don't know what they were looking for, but they were most definitely looking for something. I remember every time we sent fighters out to intercept them, they would disappear off our radar, only to reappear when the fighters were gone. They obviously weren't going anywhere until they found what they wanted to find."

Force also believes that, because of the superior technology they were witnessing, the military was scared to death of these things. "We had nukes in the area, and there was nothing we could have done if they wanted to either disable our missiles or destroy them. We were in the middle of the intelligence community in Miami during the Cold War, and these things were flying around like they could care less if we knew they were there, so these things really scared the hell out of us."

I also asked Schroeder how he felt about this becoming a life-long quest for him, and he admitted this has been the most involved investigation he has ever attempted or been involved in. As an old-school detective, he would use a storyboard to solve cases, take photos and other data and put them on a wall to look at. Eventually, an image would come to his head. He would base his case on that image. "If I do that with this case, I get more confused. There are so many sources and so much conflicting information that I had to sift through what was relevant and what was not, what was fact and what was fiction," he admitted. "Solving this 'case' of what these things were and why they were there that night has been the hardest thing I've ever undertaken."

From the outset, I always believed this case was particularly important to UFO research because of when and where it happened. In my experience, collecting corroborate, tangible evidence from reliable sources goes a long way in validating paranormal phenomena – at least from the standpoint that you can say "something" strange did indeed occur and the evidence exists to prove it. This case, I felt, had all of those criteria met.

When I asked Schroeder about the importance of this case, he was quick to verify it as such. "The incident by itself is one of thousands of reported radar sightings throughout modern history, but two things make it so important to Ufology research: a) as a military radar operator, and then as a detective, I had the experience and training to both understand what I saw and subsequently investigate the case in more detail, and b) once I opened that can of worms, I found that my part of the case was just a small piece of a much bigger picture of what was happening at the time – UFOs flying over military and missile bases, downed aircraft with casualties, military cover ups, etc.," he stressed. "The historical relevance is there as well, from the standpoint that it took place during one of the most active UFO flaps in U.S. history, it took place at the height of the Cold War, and it involved many credible witnesses. And I might add that this case isn't over. There is more to investigate here, and hopefully more information will come out sooner rather than later."

Schroeder accepts the fact some of his questions will never be answered in his lifetime, but feels he can never give up searching because of that. "You do the best work you can, and you hope someone else picks up the ball and takes it to the finish line," he said. "That will be my closure – that my work is good enough and factual enough that it will aid the next investigator and become part of the overall body of research that one day defines the work that led to ET disclosure and what is hopefully a new phase in human evolution."

And as far as whether we are alone in the universe ...

"If we were able to find out, definitively, that we are not alone in the universe, it changes everything. We are not alone. Loneliness is a terrible thing and planetary loneliness is an even more terrible thing," he said. "As Jodie Foster's character said in the movie *Contact*, 'it would be a terrible waste of space.' Nature abhors a vacuum, and we are not alone. It is going to be reassuring to most people."

Schroeder feels fortunate that he could come forward with his story and share it with others. He truly hopes it makes a difference, but what he does not realize is that it already has. As you finish this book, you are already experiencing a personal paradigm shift. You are questioning old, tired belief systems and asking yourself if working towards a newer, brighter tomorrow, where truth is transparent and information shared by everyone, is not worth striving for. You are also asking yourself: If UFOs are real and their inhabitants extraterrestrial, what might this mean for humanity? And what can we do to make sure it is good for humanity? Because of one man's courage to come forward and tell the truth, you are opening up to new possibilities … and asking more questions … and understanding … and evolving. And others will as well.

Imagine if every witness came forward and did the same.

Appendix

Even though the UFO flap in South Florida occurred almost 50 years ago, certain documents still exist that confirm not only that these incidents occurred, but also that there were several eyewitnesses to the sightings that took place during the weeks and months that followed the initial incident on the night of March 31, 1967.

These documents also reveal that the U.S. Air Force took an active interest in these sightings, as they prepared reports and press releases to address (albeit dismiss) them. When it comes to corroborating reports of UFO sightings and producing tangible evidence of their taking place, it is vitally important to gather as much documentation as possible. Bill Schroeder made it a point to track down many of these documents in his efforts to validate his experiences, and they represent important evidence as to the reality of the UFO phenomenon.

A/C (HELICOPTER) 7 Apr 67 Crestview, Fla.

DEPARTMENT OF THE AIR FORCE
HEADQUARTERS 19TH COMBAT SUPPORT GROUP (SAC)
HOMESTEAD AIR FORCE BASE, FLORIDA 33030

REPLY TO ATTN OF: BPR

4 May 1967

SUBJECT: Investigations and Findings

TO: FTD (TDETR)
Wright-Patterson AFB OH 45433

1. The following information is forwarded in accordance with AFR 80-17, para 7 a.

a. A report of UFO sightings was forwarded to Homestead AFB at 0945, 7 Apr 1967, from Crestview Elementary School located at 2201 NW 187th Street, Miami. Copies of the statements received from the three teachers are attached. (See Exhibits A, B, and C)

b. Further investigation revealed that a Coast Guard helicopter was operating in the general area around North Perry Airport, just three miles to the north of the school. Instructions were to hover no higher than 1000 feet and to perform "touch and goes" from the end of the runway. The helicopters were white with red and black markings. The maneuvers began at 0931 just fourteen minutes before the sightings were first made.

c. As the colorings corresponded fairly well to those reported, the maneuvers were in conformance to those on the attached descriptions, the range and direction of sighting are the same as that of the North Perry Airport, and the sun was in such a position as to possibly have caused reflected light to strike observers located south of any airborne objects, the Homestead AFB Office of Information, upon query demand, issued a news release on 10 April 1967. See Exhibit D.

d. Exhibits F, G and H give an accurate portrayal of both the radio stations' and newspapers' unfavorable reactions to the news release. All questions brought up subsequent to the release have not been officially answered as no further statements have been solicited from Homestead AFB by any news media. The atmosphere surrounding this incident is somewhat emotional. In fact, it appears that often times individuals reactions have been significantly influenced by their wanting to see some unidentifiable phenomena. Mass reaction to any stress situation often deviates from the norm which would be displayed had each person been isolated from those around him. Finally, once an individual unequivocally states that he saw a "Flying Saucer", normal psychological responses would tend to compel him to maintain his story against all attempts at

1003764

Crestview Air Force Report, Page 1

at logical solutions which vary from his account. The answers to such questions as "why was there no sound" and "why couldn't we see the rotors" seem obvious. Upwind observers might not even hear a jet engine run up at distances above one mile and props rotating at high RPM are hard to distinguish at close range, let alone at two to four miles.

e. In the wake of this first report, 15 separate unrelated reports were called in within a one week period. Many of these are still under investigation. Information on these will be forwarded, where applicable, as soon after investigations are completed as possible.

2. Below is listed information required by AFR 80-17 a:

Theodore J. Lynn, Jr., 1st Lt, USAF (SAC)
Base UFO Investigator
AC 305 Office Phone: 257-7327 Home Phone: 257-5403
Official Address: BPR, Homestead AFB FL 33030

FOR THE COMMANDER

THEODORE J. LYNN, JR., 1Lt, USAF
Base UFO Investigator

8 Atch
1. Exhibit A
2. Exhibit B
3. Exhibit C
4. Exhibit D
5. Exhibit E
6. Exhibit F
7. Exhibit G
8. Exhibit H

Crestview Air Force Report, Page 2

NEWS RELEASE

UNITED STATES AIR FORCE

HEADQUARTERS 19th BOMBARDMENT WING (SAC)

DIRECTORATE OF INFORMATION, HOMESTEAD AFB, FLA. 33030 (305)336-8610

HOMESTEAD AFB, Fla. (Apr 10) -- The Air Force has completed an investigation of the UFO sighting by the students and teachers of Crestview Elementary School of 2201 NW 187th St., at 9:45, April 7th.

The majority of the witnesses described the object as white with a red light that flashed once. The object was sighted along a line north-northwest of the school. Witnesses differed as to the size and distance of the object.

The investigation revealed that a Coast Guard helicopter, white with red trim, was maneuvering in the area of North Perry Airport between 9:31AM and 11:07AM the morning of the report. The helicopter was practicing landings and takeoffs in a East-West direction between ground level and 1000 feet altitude.

North Perry Airport is almost due North of the elementary school and approximately three miles in distance.

(MORE)

HOM 67-4-3

PEACE IS OUR PROFESSION

Attach D

Crestview Air Force News Release, Page 1

The Air Force concludes that given the time of the day with the angle of the Sun and the unfamiliar maneuvering of the white and red helicopter the witnesses could not identify it as such.

As to the number of objects sighted the white and red objects was the only consistent description given. The Air Force attributes the other objects to the high number of small aircraft activity in the vicinity of North Perry Airport.

-30-

Crestview Air Force News Release, Page 2

PROJECT 10073 RECORD

1. [illegible] [illegible]	2. LOCATION Opalocka, Florida — MULTIPLE
3. [illegible] [illegible]	10. CONCLUSION AIRCRAFT (Helicopter)
4. NUMBER OF OBJECTS 2	
5. LENGTH OF OBSERVATION 2-3 minutes	11. BRIEF SUMMARY AND ANALYSIS Object was red, compared to small single aircraft with flashing redlights. The flight was straight to NE, reversed courde and then straight down.
6. TYPE OF OBSERVATION Ground Visual	
7. COURSE [illegible]	
8. PHOTOS Yes X No	RETURN TO: Director Aerospace Studies Inst ATTN: Archives Branch Maxwell AFB, Alabama
9. PHYSICAL EVIDENCE Yes X No	SMC

FTD SEP 63 0-329 (TDE) Previous editions of this form may be used.

Crestview Air Force Conclusion

DEPARTMENT OF THE AIR FORCE
72ND BOMBARDMENT WING (SAC)
APO NEW YORK 09845

REPLY TO ATTN OF: DCOI

SUBJECT: UFO

1 May 1967

TO: Foreign Technology Division
Air Force Systems Command
Wright Patterson Air Force Base, Ohio

1. In accordance with the provisions of AFR 200-2, Paragraph 3, the following report is submitted on the subject sighting:

a. Description of Object:

(1) Disc shaped object with two distinct levels (upper & lower deck).

(2) Length of KC-135.

(3) Very bright - brilliant white.

(4) One (1).

(5) Not applicable.

(6) Two level appearance - reddish looking band slighly above the midsection.

(7) None.

(8) None.

(9) None.

b. Description of Course of Object:

(1) No specific item.

(2) Zero (0°) as the object appeared to be floating on the water.

(3) Forty five (45°).

(4) Object appeared to be floating or hovering just above the water and traveled a short distance from left to right and back. It then began to rise from the water traveling from right to left. At this time the picture was taken. Object then reversed its' flight path and disappeared from view.

Peace . . . . is our Profession

Ramey AFB Report, Page 1

(5) Object disappeared to the northeast.

(6) Approximately five (5) minutes.

c. Manner of Observation:

(1) Ground visual.

(2) None.

(3) Not applicable.

d. Time and Date of Sighting:

(1) 16/1000Z - 1100Z (Approximately).

e. Location of Observer:

(1) Beach - Northeast corner of Ramey Air Force Base.

f. Indentifying Information of Observer:

(1) Not applicable.

(2) [illegible]

g. Weather and Winds - Aloft Conditions at Time and Place of Sighting:

(1) Clear.

(2) Surface - @ 1000Z = 100°/5K; @ 1100Z = 130°/2K; @ 1200Z = 100°/2K;
6,000' - @ 1100Z = 080°/7K; 10,000' - @ 1100Z = 260°/7K
16,000' - @ 1100Z = Calm; 20,000' - @ 1100Z = 240/5K
30,000' - @ 1100Z = 270/37K; 50,000' - @ 1100Z = 280/36K

(3) 1000Z - 1200Z 25D E7GKI

(4) 1000Z - 1200Z 15 NM

(5) 1000Z - .9
1100Z - .7
1200Z - .8

(6) None.

Ramey AFB Report, Page 2

(7) Surface to 7500' = -17°/7500'

7500' to 10,000' = +4°/2500'

10,000' to 20,000' = -22°/10,000'

20,000' to 30,000' = -21°/10,000' All °C

30,000' to 40,000' = -24°/10,000'

40,000' to 50,000' = -18°/10,000'

Tropopause

h. None.

i. None.

j. None.

k. Robert D. Williamson, Captain, USAF, Chief, Combat Intelligence Branch, 72d Bomb Wing (SAC). Comments: It is the opinion of the preparing officer that Airman Padilla and Henry are reliable and stable individuals. They are not the publicity seeking type. Airman Padilla was particularly concerned that other people would think him a "Nut" if his sighting became public. After having discussed this sighting with other members of the Intelligence Division and letting the Prediction and Interpretation Section examine the 35 mm slide, this seems to be a creditable sighting incident.

l. One (1) 35 mm color slide taken by Airman Padilla.

ROBERT D. WILLIAMSON, Captain, USAF
UFO Representative
Intelligence Division

1 Atch
Black & White 8 X 10 inch Photo, Copied from 35mm Color Slide, 1 cy

35 mm slide

Ramey AFB. - ?
- Photo. ? -

Ramey AFB Report, Page 3

Proposed reply to letter from A2C Guillermo Padilla

Dear Airman Padilla:

Reference your recent observation and subsequent photograph of an unidentified object. Before a comprehensive photographic analysis can be made, the following camera data is necessary:

(a) Type, model and make of camera.

(b) Brand and type of film.

(c) ~~Focal length of camera~~ Speed, focal length, and make of lens.

(d) ~~Exposure time~~ Filters used,

(e) "f" stop. Lens opening used, that is

(f) Shutter speed used. ~~thanks~~

If you would forward the original slide, it will be returned upon completion of the photographic analysis.

Thank you for reporting your observation to the Air Force.

atch
W-Penelope

Ramey AFB Report, Page 4

MAY 23 1967

Dear Airman Padilla:

Reference your recent observation and subsequent photograph of an unidentified object. Before a comprehensive photographic analysis can be made, the following camera data is necessary:

(a) Type, modelf and make of camera.

(b) Brand and type of film.

(c) Speed, focal length, and make of lens.

(d) Filters used.

(e) Lens opening used, that is "f" stop.

(f) Shutter speed used.

If you would forward the original slide, it will be returned upon completion of the photographic analysis.

Thank you for reporting your observation to the Air Force.

Sincerely,

GEORGE P. FREEMAN, JR.
Lt Colonel, USAF
Chief, Civil Branch
Community Relations Division
Office of Information

Attachment (W-P envelope)

A2C Guillermo S. Padilla
72nd Bombardment Wing (SAC)
ATTN: DCOI
APO New York, New York 09845

COORDINATED BY: SAFOI-CC

SAFOIC Coord cy
Cmbk cy
Rdrs cy
Acty cy
Stbk cy

Ramey AFB Report, Page 5

Proposed reply to letter from A2C Guillermo Padilla

Dear Airman Padilla:

Reference your recent observation and subsequent photograph of an unidentified object. Before a comprehensive photographic analysis can be made, the following camera data is necessary:

(a) Type of camera

(b) Type of film

(c) Focal length of camera

(d) Exposure time

(e) "f" stop

(f) Shutter speed

If you would forward the original slide, it will be returned upon completion of the photographic analysis.

Thank you for reporting your observation to the Air Force.

Ramey AFB Report, Page 6

References

Chapter 1

Hach, Steve. 2004. National Park Service: U.S. Department of the Interior. *Cold War in South Florida: Historic Resource Study.* Cultural Resources: Southeast Region.

Mason, John W. *The Cold War, 1945-1991.* (Routledge Press, 1996).

McWilliams, John C. *The 1960s Cultural Revolution.* (Greenwood Press, 2000).

Montieth, Sharon. *American Culture in the 1960s.* (Edinburgh University Press, 2008).

Chapter 2

U.S. Army Air Defense Digest. U.S. Army Air Defense School, Fort Bliss, Texas, 1967.

Schroeder, Bill. Various Personal Interviews. 2013-2016.

Force, Dennis. Personal Interview. 12 June 2016.

Chapter 3

Gordon, Yefim. *Mikoyan MiG-21 (Famous Russian Aircraft).* (Midland Press, 2008).

Eden, Paul. *The Encyclopedia of Modern Military Aircraft.* (Amber Books, 2004).

Greenwood, Barry and Fawcett, Lawrence. *Clear Intent: The Government Coverup of the UFO Experience.* (Prentice Hall Trade, 1984).

Chapter 4

Schroeder, Bill. Various Personal Interviews. 2013-2016.

Force, Dennis. Personal Interview. 12 June 2016.

Chapter 5

Department of the Air Force. Investigations and Findings Report. May 1, 1967. 72nd Bombardment Wing (SAC). Robert D. Williamson, Captain, USAF, UFO Representative, Intelligence Division.

NUFORC Sighting Report. May 5, 1967.

NUFORC Sighting Report. April 1, 1967.

Chapter 6

APRO Bulletin. May-June 1967.

Barry, Bill. 1967. Return of the UFO. *The Miami News,* 13 April.

Petit, Mike. 1967. 10 Chaotic Minutes, and the Kids Screamed. *The Miami Herald,* 8 April.

Bruning, Fred. 1967. AF Says "It" Was Copter; People Who Saw It Say No. *The Miami Herald,* 11 April.

Allen, William. 1967. Hundreds See Flying Saucers Over Miami. *National Enquirer.* 25 June.

Children Contend: "Air Force Wrong About Dade UFO." *Homestead News Leader.* 11 April 1967.

United States Air Force News Release. April 10, 1967. Headquarters 19th Bombardment Wing (SAC), Directorate of Information, Homestead AFB, FLA.

Department of the Air Force. Investigations and Findings Report. May 4, 1967. Headquarters 19th Combat Support Group (SAC). Theodore J. Lynn, 1st Lt. USAF, Homestead AFB UFO Investigator.

Lorenzen, Coral E. 1968. *UFOs over the Americas.* New York: Signet Books.

NUFORC Sighting Report. April 1, 1967.

Chapter 7

Project Blue Book. Annual Report, USAF. 1968.

Hall, Richard H. 1978. Abstract. *1967: The Overlooked UFO Wave and the Colorado Project.*

Bloecher, Ted. August 31, 1974. *Inventory of TRB Catalog of Type 7-8 References, 1897 to 1974.* Unpublished.

Webb, David. May 1976. *1973 – Year of the Humanoids.* Illinois Center for UFO Studies.

Hobana, Ion, and Weverbergh, J. 1975. *UFOs from Behind the Iron Curtain.* New York: Bantam Books.

Stanway, Roger H., and Pace, A.R. 1968. *Flying Saucer Report.* England: Newcastle Observatory.

Department of Energy, Nevada Operations Office. *United States Nuclear Tests: July 1945 through September 1992.*

The National Security Archive Electronic Briefing Book No. 197. August 18, 2006. *How Many and Where Were the Nukes?* Edited by William Burr.

MUFON Report. MUFON, MUJ-345, 15. Case ID: 1017. Source: Robert Salas.

Salas, Robert, and Klotz, James. 2005. *Faded Giant: The 1967 Missile/UFO Incidents.* BookSurge, LLC.

"Who Speaks for Earth?" *Cosmos: A Personal Voyage.* PBS. 1980. Television.

Salas, Robert. Personal Interview. 4 June 2016.

MUFON Report. MUFON Case ID: 64749. 1967 – NC Auxiliary Bombing Range Incident.

NICAP. "The 1967 UFO Chronology: The Mother of All Sighting Waves."

Shevardnadze, Sophie. Interview with Paul Hellyer. RT News. 17 January 2014.

Chapter 8

Yun, Liu. 2000. *Regional Surface Temperature Inversion.* Meteorological Press.

Winkler, David F. and Webster, Julie L. June 1997. *Searching the Skies: The Legacy of the United States Cold War Defense Radar Program.* (Report) U.S. Army Construction Engineering Research Laboratories.

NICAP. "The 1967 UFO Chronology: The Mother of All Sighting Waves."

Watson, Raymond C. 2009. *Radar Origins Worldwide.* Trafford Publishing.

Buderi, Robert. 1996. *The Invention that Changed the World.* New York: Simon & Schuster.

Walker, Martin. 1995. *The Cold War: A History.* New York: Holt Paperbacks.

Winkler, David F. 1997. *Searching the Skies: The Legacy of the United States Cold War Defense Radar System*. United States Air Force Combat Command.

Woodward, Joan. "The Washington, DC, Area Jet Chase of July 26, 2002." *International UFO Reporter*. Winter 2002-2003. Vol. 27. No. 4.

Hanlon, Chris. "UFO Sighting by RAF Pilot Dubbed 'Saucer Sam' in 1952 Left Aviation Minister Convinced We Are Not Alone." *The Daily Mail*, United Kingdom. 27 May, 2012. Web.

Thayer, Gordon D. 1971. "The Lakenheath Radar/Visual UFO Case." *Journal of Astronautics and Aeronautics*. September 1971.

McDonald, J.E. 1970. "UFOs over Lakenheath in 1956." *Flying Saucer Review*. Vol. 16. No. 2.

"The Kaikoura UFO Sighting Continues to Baffle, 30 Years On." *Newshub.co*. MediaWorks TV. Web. 20 October 2008.

Maccabee, Bruce. March-April 1987. "The Fantastic Flight of JAL 1628." *International UFO Reporter*. Vol. 12. No. 2

Bernton, Hal. March 6, 1987. "FAA Has No Conclusion About UFO." *Anchorage Daily News* (Anchorage).

Abrassart, J.M. 2010. "The Beginning of the Belgian UFO Wave." *SUNlite*. Vol. 2. No. 6.

"Famous UFO Cases: The 2004 Mexican UFO Incident." *Latest UFO Sightings*. Web. 14 April 2010.

Speigel, Lee. "UFO Encounters with Airplanes: Pilots, Officials Discuss Potential Safety Hazards." *Huffington Post*. Web. 12 April 2012.

Chapter 9

Keyhoe, Donald E. "What Radar Tells About Flying Saucers." *True, The Man's Magazine*. December 1952. Print.

Keyhoe, Donald E. "Radar Tracks Blips and Blobs." *The True Report on Flying Saucers.* 1967. Print

Salas, Robert. Personal Interview. 4 June 2016.

Schroeder, Bill. Various Personal Interviews. 2013-2016.

Kloetzke, Chase. Personal Interview. 12 May 2016.

Chapter 10

Salas, Robert. Personal Interview. 4 June 2016.

Schroeder, Bill. Various Personal Interviews. 2013-2016.

Kloetzke, Chase. Personal Interview. 12 May 2016.

Force, Dennis. Personal Interview. 12 June 2016.

Afterword

Schroeder, Bill. Various Personal Interviews. 2013-2016.

Force, Dennis. Personal Interview. 12 June 2016.

Biographies

JACK ROTH is a veteran writer and investigative journalist who has spent the past two decades researching and documenting unexplained phenomena, including hauntings, UFO sightings and alien abductions. He initially went down the "rabbit hole" known as paranormal research in 1995 when he took some life-changing photographs at a haunted plantation in Louisiana. Since then, he has felt compelled to search for the answers to some of life's biggest mysteries. He conducted seven years of research for his first book, *Ghost Soldiers of Gettysburg*, in which he and co-author Patrick Burke meticulously documented both the battle history and paranormal legacy of one of America's most celebrated historical sites.

Jack's innate curiosity and attention to detail have helped him develop an extensive network of contacts in the world of paranormal studies, which ultimately led him to another important project — a feature-length documentary titled *extraordinary: the stan romanek story*. By producing this award-winning film, he helped bring to the public consciousness one of the most fascinating and well-documented cases of alien abduction and alien/human hybridization in U.S. history. Jack considers his quest a journey of enlightenment, and his goal is to continue to document his research and experiences for the benefit of those who continue to live in the shadows of secrecy and for the hope of a brighter future for humanity.

***

After completing his military service, BILL SCHROEDER attended the Tampa Police Academy in 1972 and graduated second in his class. He would later go on to become a major crimes investigator, homicide detective and FBI trained hostage negotiator. He served in several law enforcement agencies and attended numerous academies over the years, where he also trained officers in Boston, New Hampshire, New Jersey, Maine and Florida. In 1979, he served as a personal bodyguard to the Shah of Iran during his exile in the Bahamas and Mexico.

After his retirement in 1990, Bill started his own private investigation firm, Tampa PI, which quickly became one of the most prestigious agencies in the state. Bill closed his agency in 2011 and now dedicates his life to the world of Ufology and the quest for the truth.

***

MAURIZIO BAIATA is an Italian investigative reporter, magazine editor and UFO researcher. After an intense publishing life with several rock music magazines, including the *Rolling Stone*

Italian edition, he moved to New York City in the to work as a radio correspondent for RAI TV and as editor for the daily *Il Progresso Italo Americano*. After moving back to Italy in the 1990s, Maurizio became a full-time UFO journalist, producing and editing documentaries, multimedia encyclopedias, and UFO magazines. He also translated and released two books by Col. Philip Corso. In 2009, he moved to Phoenix, AZ, where he founded and acted as editor in chief for the bi-monthly *Open Minds Magazine*. Recognized as a leading authority in the field of Ufology, Maurizio has lectured worldwide and appeared as a guest on countless TV and radio shows. He published his first book, *The Aliens Saved My Life*, in 2011.